Curri**cul**m Focus

The invaders

HOPSCOTCH
EDUCATIONAL PUBLISHING

Curriculum Focus series

History

Famous Events
Famous People
Invaders
Toys
Tudors

Geography

Islands and Seasides
The Local Area

Science

Ourselves
Animals, Plants and Habitats: Key Stage 1
Materials: Key Stage 1

Published by Hopscotch Educational Publishing Ltd,
Unit 2, The Old Brushworks, 56 Pickwick Road,
Corsham, Wilts SN13 9BX
Tel: 01249 701701

© 2003 Hopscotch Educational Publishing

Written by Christine Moorcroft
Linked ICT activities by Michelle Singleton
Series design by Blade Communications
Illustrated by Jane Bottomley
Cover illustration by Virginia Gray
Printed by Clintplan, Southam

Christine Moorcroft hereby asserts her moral right to be
identified as the author of this work in accordance with
the Copyright, Designs and Patents Act, 1988.

ISBN 1-904307-55-8

Contents

Cross-curricular links

Chapter	History SoW	Geography SoW	PSHE and Citizenship	Literacy framework	Numeracy framework	ICT SoW
1	Units 6A, 6B, 6C	Unit 9	1a, 2e, 2i, 4b, 5g Units 5, 12	Y3, Term 2, T10, T13, T17 Y4, Term 2, T21, T22		Units 3a, 4a
2	Unit 6A	Unit 9	2e, 2k, 4b Unit 5	Y3, Term 1, T21 Y4, Term 2, T23		Unit 4b
3	Unit 6A	Unit 9	4b Units 5, 8	Y3, Term 2, T17 Y3, Term 3, T13 Y4, Term 2, T21, T23		Units 3a, 3c
4	Unit 6A	Unit 9	4b Unit 5	Y3, Term 3, T17 Y4, Term 2, T17, T23	Roman numerals	Unit 4a
5	Unit 6B	Unit 9	Unit 5	Y3, all terms, S6 Y4, all terms, S3 Y3, Term 2, S17		Unit 3d
6	Unit 6B	Unit 9	Units 5, 11	Y3, Term 3, T25 Y4, Term 1, T12, T24		Units 3a, 4a
7	Unit 6B	Unit 9	Unit 5	Y3, Term 1, T13 Y3, Term 2, T17 Y4, Term 2, T16		Units 3a, 4a
8	Unit 6C	Unit 9	Units 5, 11	Y3, Term 3, T13 Y4, Term 2, T16		Unit 3e
9	Unit 6C	Unit 9	Unit 5	Y3, Term 2, T14 Y4, Term 1, T27		Unit 4a
10	Unit 6C	Unit 9	Unit 5	Y3, Term 1, S11		Unit 4a
11	Unit 6C	Unit 9	Unit 5	Y3, Term 1, S10, S11 Y4, Term 2, T16		Unit 3c

Introduction

Curriculum Focus: Invaders helps to make history fun by giving you (especially those of you who are not history specialists) the support you need to plan stimulating and exciting lessons. It helps you to plan and teach a unit of work based on the QCA exemplar scheme of work for history at Key Stage 2 and, where appropriate, gives indications as to how the work can be linked with other areas of the curriculum.

The book gives you a sound foundation from which to plan a unit of work for your class. It includes:

- detailed **Teachers' notes** giving background information on each topic and/or the concept to be taught
- fully illustrated **Generic sheets** offering a wealth of reusable resource material
- a **Lesson plan** full of ideas for introducing and developing the lesson
- photocopiable and differentiated **Activity sheets** to support individual and group work

Any unit of work on the peoples who have invaded and settled in Britain will be enlivened by visits to museums and other sites, and sources such as artefacts (including replicas), photographs, works of art and documents. Therefore, at the end of the book you will find a list of publications, museums and websites from which materials can be obtained. The book also offers suggestions for ways in which you can help children to learn from primary and secondary sources, and ideas for helping the children to record what they find out.

Chapter 1 should be used to introduce a unit of work on any group of invaders. The other chapters of the book are arranged in three sections:

- Chapters 2–4: A Roman case study
- Chapters 5–7: An Anglo-Saxon case study
- Chapters 8–11: A Viking case study.

The material in each chapter is designed to be used flexibly and not necessarily consecutively with the whole class.

Curriculum Focus: Invaders recognises that there will be different levels of attainment among the children and that their developing reading skills will require different levels of support during individual and group work. To help you to provide activities that meet the needs of your class, each chapter contains three photocopiable sheets based on the same material but for children of different levels of attainment. This enables the whole class to take part in a similar activity.

- Activity sheet 1 in each chapter is intended for lower attaining children.
- Activity sheet 2 should be suitable for most children.
- Activity sheet 3 challenges the higher attaining children.

A key source of information about the Anglo-Saxons and the Viking invasion and settlement is the *Anglo-Saxon Chronicle*, which was compiled over several centuries ending in 1154.

Contemporary and near-contemporary written sources about Roman Britain include the writings of Julius Caesar (*c.*102/100–44BC) and the historians Cassius Dio (*c.*150–*c.*235) and Tacitus (*c.*55–120).

At the end of the book there is a glossary for each chapter, followed by a list of useful resources.

Ask the children to find out as much as they can about why people move to live in different places. Give them resources such as leaflets from estate agents, job advertisements and newspaper articles, past and present, about emigrants, immigrants, refugees and asylum seekers. Ask them to make notes about the reasons why people migrate under three main headings:

• Looking for a better life
• Finding work
• Escaping from fear or persecution

Tell the children they are now going to look in more detail at the reasons why people move.

Group activities

Activity sheet 1

This sheet is for children who can write captions and are learning to use secondary sources, such as illustrations, to find out about a situation. They can relate what they find out to their previous learning. They have to look at pictures of places from which people moved, and decide what was happening there. They are asked to write why people might move from that situation.

Activity sheet 2

This sheet is for children who can interpret written sources to find the information they are looking for and are learning to identify and summarise the main points. They have to read what people have said about their moves, and classify the reasons under the headings given.

Activity sheet 3

This sheet is for children who are learning how to carry out research to find specific information and, with help, can ask the appropriate questions. They can classify and record their findings on a chart. They have to carry out a survey among people known to them to find out why they moved, and then classify the reasons, using the given headings.

Plenary session

Invite some of the children who completed Activity sheet 1 to share the captions they wrote for the pictures. Discuss any differences and why there could be more than one reason for people moving from their homes in some situations (for example, a new job can also bring a better way of life, as can escaping from fear or persecution).

Make a large copy of the chart at the bottom of Activity sheet 2. Ask some of those who completed this sheet to read out what the people said about moving home, and give those who completed other activities the opportunity to contribute to the chart.

Invite some of the children who completed Activity sheet 3 to talk about what they did and their main findings. Ask them to display their work after the lesson for others to read later.

Ideas for support

A teaching assistant or other adult could work with the children who need help in reading the text in Activity sheet 1, first giving them the opportunity to say what they think is happening, to predict what the text might say and to identify any words they recognise.

The children who work on Activity sheet 2 could support one another by taking turns to read aloud the words of the people depicted and to help one another with difficult words.

Ideas for extension

Ask the children if any of their names come from other countries and what that shows about people in their families in the past. Tell them that some surnames show from what part of Britain a family originated. Some surnames come from particular parts of Britain and, although they have spread over the country as people have moved, they are still more common in their places of origin than in other places. Examples include Abercromby ('mouth of the crooked stream') in Fife, Scotland; Cavill ('jackdaw field') from East Yorkshire; Holman ('dweller in a hollow') from Sussex; Surtees ('on the River Tees') from County Durham.

Linked ICT activities

Collect images of houses and buildings (from magazines, estate agents' details or locally using a digital camera; for fun, you could include a local stately home or castle). Using a desktop publishing program such as *Textease* or Microsoft *Publisher*, create a sales flyer to contain an image (see Useful resources on page 127).

Ask the children to choose a picture of a building. Ask them to think about who might live in the property and why they are moving out.

Introduction

Curriculum Focus: Invaders helps to make history fun by giving you (especially those of you who are not history specialists) the support you need to plan stimulating and exciting lessons. It helps you to plan and teach a unit of work based on the QCA exemplar scheme of work for history at Key Stage 2 and, where appropriate, gives indications as to how the work can be linked with other areas of the curriculum.

The book gives you a sound foundation from which to plan a unit of work for your class. It includes:

- detailed **Teachers' notes** giving background information on each topic and/or the concept to be taught
- fully illustrated **Generic sheets** offering a wealth of reusable resource material
- a **Lesson plan** full of ideas for introducing and developing the lesson
- photocopiable and differentiated **Activity sheets** to support individual and group work

Any unit of work on the peoples who have invaded and settled in Britain will be enlivened by visits to museums and other sites, and sources such as artefacts (including replicas), photographs, works of art and documents. Therefore, at the end of the book you will find a list of publications, museums and websites from which materials can be obtained. The book also offers suggestions for ways in which you can help children to learn from primary and secondary sources, and ideas for helping the children to record what they find out.

Chapter 1 should be used to introduce a unit of work on any group of invaders. The other chapters of the book are arranged in three sections:

- Chapters 2–4: A Roman case study
- Chapters 5–7: An Anglo-Saxon case study
- Chapters 8–11: A Viking case study.

The material in each chapter is designed to be used flexibly and not necessarily consecutively with the whole class.

Curriculum Focus: Invaders recognises that there will be different levels of attainment among the children and that their developing reading skills will require different levels of support during individual and group work. To help you to provide activities that meet the needs of your class, each chapter contains three photocopiable sheets based on the same material but for children of different levels of attainment. This enables the whole class to take part in a similar activity.

- Activity sheet 1 in each chapter is intended for lower attaining children.
- Activity sheet 2 should be suitable for most children.
- Activity sheet 3 challenges the higher attaining children.

A key source of information about the Anglo-Saxons and the Viking invasion and settlement is the *Anglo-Saxon Chronicle*, which was compiled over several centuries ending in 1154.

Contemporary and near-contemporary written sources about Roman Britain include the writings of Julius Caesar (*c.*102/100–44BC) and the historians Cassius Dio (*c.*150–*c.*235) and Tacitus (*c.*55–120).

At the end of the book there is a glossary for each chapter, followed by a list of useful resources.

People on the move

Reasons for people to be on the move

People move from the place where they were born or grew up for various reasons. Generic sheets 1 and 2 (pages 10 and 11) summarise the reasons and can be used as starting points for discussion. Bring the examples into the discussions and supplement them with others from recent news items and from the children's experiences.

Individuals and groups of people move within Britain, into Britain and out of Britain. Their migration can be thought of in relation to feelings of:

- fear (of persecution or war)
- despair (caused by poverty, famine and other disasters)
- hope (of finding work, improving their standard of living or quality of life)
- ambition (finding a better job, making a fortune or exploiting opportunities for trade or business).

Some moves are a natural stage in people's lives – for example, when young people leave home to get married or go to university. There are also people who are forced to move by others when their homes or land are taken over for industrial, commercial or other reasons – for example, when reservoirs, roads or airports are built or landowners change the use of the land, as in the Highland Clearances in Scotland.

Invasion for settlement

Invasion is more than a mass movement of a large group of people. It is an attempt to take over part or the whole of another country because that country offers something which the homeland does not – for example, land, mineral, agricultural, fishing, labour or other resources. Alternatively, the invading nation may want to enlarge its domain or build an empire (for example, the Roman Empire, the Ottoman Empire and the British Empire). Sometimes religion or politics have motivated invasion – the invading nation wants to establish its religious or political power over a larger area and a greater number of people.

The chapters that follow this one focus on invasion rather than migration. The children need to understand the difference, although there are similarities in the motives of ordinary people who settle in the conquered area after the invasion – to start a new life.

People on the move

LESSON PLAN

History objectives (Units 6A, 6B and 6C)
- To relate their own experience to the concept of settlement.
- To recognise that people have been moving between different areas for a long time, and that some reasons for moving were the same as those of people alive today.

Resources

- Brochures and advertisements from removal companies and leaflets from estate agents
- Employment advertisements from newspapers (including some with relocation packages)
- Newspaper articles about refugees and asylum seekers
- Street maps of the local area and maps of Britain and the world
- Generic sheets 1–3 (pages 10–12)
- Activity sheets 1–3 (pages 13–15)

Starting points: *whole class*

Show the children a picture of a removal van and ask them what it brings to mind. Invite them to share their experiences of moving house and ask them where they moved from and to. Help them to identify the places on the appropriate maps. Ask them about the differences and similarities between where they live now and where they lived before.

Ask the children if they know why their families moved. This needs sensitive handling if any children have moved house because of their parents' divorce or another misfortune. Talk about the reasons why people move house – for example, they want a bigger or more attractive house, a garden, a quieter neighbourhood or a different type of area. They might also move to make travelling to and from work or school easier, or they might want to move away from an area where there is a high crime rate, noise or other nuisances. The children might also have experience of moving because one of their parents finds a job in another area or is relocated at work.

Show the children newspaper articles about refugees and asylum seekers and encourage them to think about the experiences of these people. Read some of the articles and ask the children what has made these people leave their countries to come to

Britain. Help them to find the countries on a map of the world.

Introduce the words 'immigrant', 'immigrate' and 'immigration' in relation to people moving to Britain from other countries. The children could talk about their own experiences of immigration or about members of their families who are or were immigrants.

Introduce the words 'emigrant', 'emigrate' and 'emigration'. On a map of the world, point out the countries to which many British people moved, especially in the early- and mid-twentieth century – for example, Australia, Canada, New Zealand and Zimbabwe. Discuss what made people emigrate from Britain at that time (for further research, search a source such as the *Daily Mail Century* CD-Rom for newspaper articles from the period). Generic sheets 1 and 2 provide useful summaries.

Give the children copies of Generic sheet 3 and read the text with them. Ask them if they or other people in their families have family names that come from other countries. Discuss why most of Ella's grandfather's family stayed in Hungary, despite the revolution, and why many other people remain in a country despite wars, natural disasters or upheavals. Draw out the idea that for many people their home is where they want to be, whatever happens in or around it. You could link this with British news features in which people were reluctant to leave their homes even if they were flooded or were to be demolished to make way for new roads or airport runways.

Ask the children what made Ella's grandfather leave Hungary, and talk about the opportunities in Britain for people to find work. Did anyone in their families come to Britain to find work, or do they know anyone who did so?

Ask the children to find out as much as they can about why people move to live in different places. Give them resources such as leaflets from estate agents, job advertisements and newspaper articles, past and present, about emigrants, immigrants, refugees and asylum seekers. Ask them to make notes about the reasons why people migrate under three main headings:

- Looking for a better life
- Finding work
- Escaping from fear or persecution

Tell the children they are now going to look in more detail at the reasons why people move.

Group activities

Activity sheet 1
This sheet is for children who can write captions and are learning to use secondary sources, such as illustrations, to find out about a situation. They can relate what they find out to their previous learning. They have to look at pictures of places from which people moved, and decide what was happening there. They are asked to write why people might move from that situation.

Activity sheet 2
This sheet is for children who can interpret written sources to find the information they are looking for and are learning to identify and summarise the main points. They have to read what people have said about their moves, and classify the reasons under the headings given.

Activity sheet 3
This sheet is for children who are learning how to carry out research to find specific information and, with help, can ask the appropriate questions. They can classify and record their findings on a chart. They have to carry out a survey among people known to them to find out why they moved, and then classify the reasons, using the given headings.

Plenary session

Invite some of the children who completed Activity sheet 1 to share the captions they wrote for the pictures. Discuss any differences and why there could be more than one reason for people moving from their homes in some situations (for example, a new job can also bring a better way of life, as can escaping from fear or persecution).

Make a large copy of the chart at the bottom of Activity sheet 2. Ask some of those who completed this sheet to read out what the people said about moving home, and give those who completed other activities the opportunity to contribute to the chart.

Invite some of the children who completed Activity sheet 3 to talk about what they did and their main findings. Ask them to display their work after the lesson for others to read later.

Ideas for support

A teaching assistant or other adult could work with the children who need help in reading the text in Activity sheet 1, first giving them the opportunity to say what they think is happening, to predict what the text might say and to identify any words they recognise.

The children who work on Activity sheet 2 could support one another by taking turns to read aloud the words of the people depicted and to help one another with difficult words.

Ideas for extension

Ask the children if any of their names come from other countries and what that shows about people in their families in the past. Tell them that some surnames show from what part of Britain a family originated. Some surnames come from particular parts of Britain and, although they have spread over the country as people have moved, they are still more common in their places of origin than in other places. Examples include Abercromby ('mouth of the crooked stream') in Fife, Scotland; Cavill ('jackdaw field') from East Yorkshire; Holman ('dweller in a hollow') from Sussex; Surtees ('on the River Tees') from County Durham.

Linked ICT activities

Collect images of houses and buildings (from magazines, estate agents' details or locally using a digital camera; for fun, you could include a local stately home or castle). Using a desktop publishing program such as Textease or Microsoft Publisher, create a sales flyer to contain an image (see Useful resources on page 127).

Ask the children to choose a picture of a building. Ask them to think about who might live in the property and why they are moving out.

Ask the children to complete a flyer by writing under three headings: a description of the property; a description of who lives there; why they are moving out. These sections could be completed at different times, to give the children practice in saving and reloading their work. Encourage them to reread the previous section before they continue writing.

You could create word banks of descriptive words, using *Textease*, to support the children's writing.

After completing their text, the children should insert the picture: scanning from a paper source, pasting in from a website (found under adult supervision) or using a digital camera.

People on the move

Work

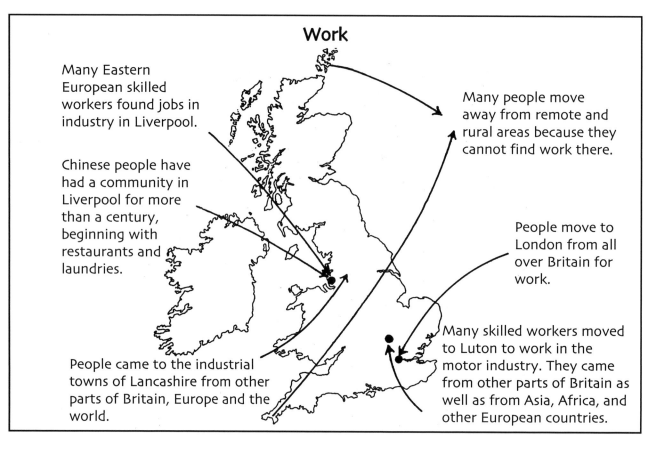

Many Eastern European skilled workers found jobs in industry in Liverpool.

Chinese people have had a community in Liverpool for more than a century, beginning with restaurants and laundries.

Many people move away from remote and rural areas because they cannot find work there.

People move to London from all over Britain for work.

People came to the industrial towns of Lancashire from other parts of Britain, Europe and the world.

Many skilled workers moved to Luton to work in the motor industry. They came from other parts of Britain as well as from Asia, Africa, and other European countries.

Starting a new life

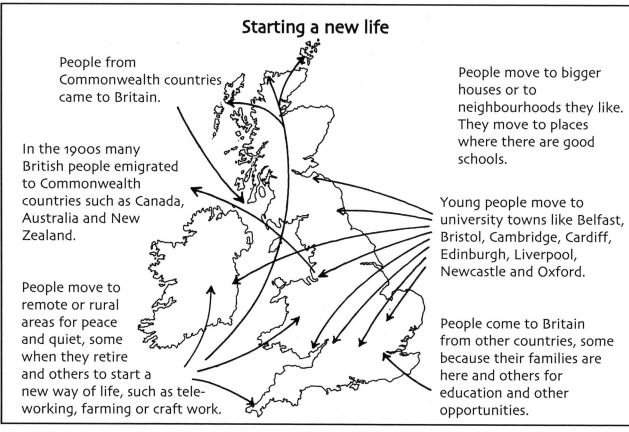

People from Commonwealth countries came to Britain.

In the 1900s many British people emigrated to Commonwealth countries such as Canada, Australia and New Zealand.

People move to remote or rural areas for peace and quiet, some when they retire and others to start a new way of life, such as tele-working, farming or craft work.

People move to bigger houses or to neighbourhoods they like. They move to places where there are good schools.

Young people move to university towns like Belfast, Bristol, Cambridge, Cardiff, Edinburgh, Liverpool, Newcastle and Oxford.

People come to Britain from other countries, some because their families are here and others for education and other opportunities.

PHOTOCOPIABLE

People on the move

Escaping from fear, war or persecution

Some people move within their neighbourhoods to get away from crime, noisy neighbours or other nuisances.

Some people moved away from Northern Ireland in the late twentieth century to avoid the Troubles.

Many European Jews came to Britain after the Second World War. They arrived in ports such as Liverpool, London and Newcastle.

Refugees and asylum seekers are still arriving in ports on the south coast from many parts of the world.

People on the move

Ella's Hungarian grandfather

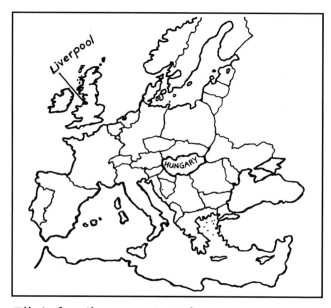

Ella's family name is Kalmar – a Hungarian name – but she was born in Liverpool and that is where she lives. Her mother and father were born in Liverpool too, but her father's father – Ella's grandfather John ('Nagypapa') – was born and grew up in a small village in Hungary.

Nagypapa's family had a farm. They had plenty of land and enough to eat, but they were not rich and they led a very simple life. But in 1956, when Nagypapa was 22, there was a revolution in Hungary: workers all over the country marched into the cities and rebelled against the government. They planned to take over and run the country. During the fighting many thousands of people were killed.

Nagypapa's family carried on farming as before, but he wanted to make a new life for himself. He and some of his friends had heard that in Britain many new factories were opening to make cars and electrical goods and that the factories needed workers.

So he and a few of his friends filled in all the forms that allowed them to emigrate to Britain. When they arrived they heard that a new factory in Liverpool needed workers, so that is where they went. At first they lived in a camp that was once used by the army. They enjoyed learning new skills and a new language, and they soon got used to living in a big city – in fact they enjoyed it.

Nagypapa met Gran (Margaret) at the factory and they were married in 1958 and bought a house in Liverpool. They had two children: Joseph, Ella's dad, and his sister Susan. They all visit their family in Hungary, who still lead a simple life and think that Nagypapa must be a millionaire because he wears a suit and has a car! He thinks they are rich because they have a lot of land.

PHOTOCOPIABLE

Name _____

People on the move

Why might these people move to live somewhere else?
Write a caption underneath each picture. Choose from:

| for a better life | for work | because of fear or persecution |

On the back of this sheet, write about what is happening in one
of the pictures.

People on the move

What made these people's families move to live somewhere else?
Fill in the chart by ticking the correct boxes.

My great-great-grandfather rented a farm in Cheshire. His two eldest sons took over the farm, but there were three other sons and two daughters. My great-grandfather was the youngest. He went to Manchester where he became an engineer on the railways.

Gemma, age 7

We moved from Grey Street to Green Close. Our new house is bigger than the old one and it has a garden. Mum says the neighbourhood is nicer.

Alan, age 7

Danayal, age 7

My grandfather was born in Pakistan. He came to Newcastle in 1958, when he was 20. He worked in a factory and was able to send money to his family every month.

I have a pen friend in the USA. His family moved there from Kilhope in County Durham in 1860. They had worked in the lead mines there. The work was hard and they had little money. Many people from the lead mining areas emigrated to the USA at that time.

Helen, age 7

An ancestor of mine went to California in the USA in 1849 when he heard that people were finding gold in the rivers and could make a lot of money from it.

Ryan, age 8

My friend's mum came to England in 1968 from Vietnam. There was a war in Vietnam from 1955 to 1975.

Sita, age 8

Name	Reason for moving		
	A better life	Work	Fear or persecution
Gemma's great-grandfather	☐	☐	☐
Alan's mum	☐	☐	☐
Danayal's grandfather	☐	☐	☐
Helen's pen friend's family	☐	☐	☐
Ryan's ancestor	☐	☐	☐
Sita's friend's mum	☐	☐	☐

Name _____

People on the move

Collect information about people you know who have moved to live in a different place. Fill in the chart.

Names	Where they moved from	Where they moved to	Reason

How many people moved for each reason below?

A better life _____   Work _____

Fear or persecution _____   Other reasons _____

In your survey, what is the most common reason for moving?

_____

_____

CHAPTER 2

Britons and Romans

The Britons

The inhabitants of Britain before the Roman invasion were developing a highly civilised society. They were certainly not savages, as some Roman writers described them; to the Romans the word 'civilised' meant literally 'dwelling in a city'.

Unlike the Romans, the Britons did not have a written form for their language. Instead, they set great store on the learning of poetry and stories; their culture was passed on orally. There was no universal language in Britain – different forms of Celtic languages were spoken in different areas.

Many of the people were indigenous inhabitants, joined by Celts who had migrated from mainland Europe from about 500BC; so the term 'Britons' is a more accurate description for the entire population than 'Celts'. The Britons lived in tribal settlements or villages, each of which usually had a fortified area – sometimes the home of the chief or leader of the tribe, or other prominent families; or the fortifications might surround an entire village.

Many of these fortifications were on hilltops while others were surrounded by an earthen bank and a ditch or fence, or built on an island in a lake. In Scotland, tall windowless towers called 'brochs' were used as places of refuge when necessary – for example, the Broch of Mousa in Shetland and of Gurness in Orkney. Examples of the remains of Iron Age hillforts that can be seen in Britain include Danebury in Hampshire and Maiden Castle in Dorset.

The Britons lived in tribal settlements, each tribe ruling an area of the country. (See Generic sheet 1 on page 21.) The tribes fought against one another at times, and the boundaries of the tribal territories shifted. However, they were not continually at war, as suggested by some Roman contemporary writers. The tribes also traded with one another.

The homes of most Britons were made of wattle (woven branches and twigs) plastered with daub (mud or clay). A few huts were built from stones, and the roofs were thatched. In Scotland many large dwellings (called 'crannogs') were built on lakes and supported by alder poles pushed into the lake bed. (See Generic sheet 1 on page 21.) These housed extended family groups. A bridge (which could be pulled up at night, like a drawbridge) linked the crannog to land. Debris from the dwelling built up on the bed of the lake and often the crannog would become an island. Many of them were still inhabited hundreds of years later.

The Britons hunted for food but they also kept domesticated animals such as sheep, cows and pigs, and grew crops. They used iron to make tools, utensils and weapons, and bronze for items such as mirrors. They also made intricately worked jewellery as well as coins from gold, silver and bronze. They wove cloth from wool and made garments such as dresses, tunics and trousers from it. Men wore short or long checked or plaid trousers and women wore long dresses of the same material. Both men and women wore woollen cloaks in cold weather. Their shoes were made from leather, with uppers stitched onto the soles. The Britons exported grain, wool, hunting dogs, slaves and metals such as tin, bronze and iron. Archaeologists have found that the Britons used a plant called soapwort for washing, and Roman sources comment on the cleanliness and tidiness of the Britons.

The Romans

The Roman Empire began in the ancient state that centred on the city of Rome; a republic was founded in 509BC, and then extended to form an empire from 27BC across Italy, through Europe and to parts of Africa and Asia, where the Romans had introduced their own customs and language (Latin).

The Romans built towns with buildings made of stone, with plastered or tiled walls. The finest buildings had mosaic floors. They built bathhouses and introduced plumbing systems to supply water for bathing and drinking. The men wore belted tunics reaching to their knees while high-ranking men wore togas. Both men and women wore leather sandals or shoes, depending on the weather.

The Roman invasions

Much of our information about the early Britons and the Roman invasions comes from Roman written sources (see Generic sheet 2 on page 22), such as the journal of Julius Caesar and the writings of the historians Tacitus and Dio Cassius. Tacitus described Britain as 'worth conquering'; he referred to its mild climate in which 'anything except vines and olives would grow' and noted the abundance of minerals, including silver and gold. A Roman writer known to the Elizabethans as 'the panegyrist of Constantine' wrote that 'the forests were without savage beasts and the ground voyd of noisome serpents. Contrariwise an infinite multitude there is of tame cattle with udders strutting full of milke'.

Historians suggest that Julius Caesar saw an invasion of Britain from his nearby base in Gaul (France) as an opportunity to increase his standing in Rome, where he shared power with the two other members of the Triumvirate, Pompey and Crassus.

Romans and Britons in battle

In battle the Britons used slings and stones, spears and long swords (used in a slashing action). Many warriors fought with no armour, but others protected themselves with wooden shields faced with leather or bronze. Some of them rode in two-wheeled horse-drawn chariots, which the Romans had never seen before. Warriors would create a fierce, aggressive appearance by painting their bodies with the blue dye woad and liming their hair into stiff spiky manes.

Julius Caesar led the first Roman invasion of Britain in 55BC, but lost many of his ships in storms. Those that landed were repelled by the Britons. Caesar prepared for his return. Back in northern Italy he built a new fleet of warships and transports which could be sailed or pulled with rows of great oars – in effect, landing craft that could be run onto the beaches in order to bring ashore men, horses and supplies. He came back in 54BC with more than 800 ships and a bigger army.

Caesar had studied and analysed the fighting methods of the Britons. His journal records:

'The manner of fighting from chariots is as follows. First of all they drive in all directions and hurl missiles. When they have worked their way in between the troops of cavalry they leap down from their chariots and fight on foot. Meanwhile the charioteers retire gradually from the combat, and dispose the chariots in such a fashion that, if the warriors are hard pressed by the host of the enemy, they may have ready means of retirement to their own side.'

By this time several British tribes had united under one king, Cassivellaunus, who is thought to have been the king of the Catuvellauni. The Romans tracked down and captured the stronghold of Cassivellaunus. Cassivellaunus accepted terms of surrender (the giving of hostages and an annual tribute payment to Rome). The Romans did not stay in Britain, but they made agreements with several tribes, including the Trinovantes of Essex.

After that, large British settlements developed in the south-east of the country and became the strongholds of local kings and chiefs. These settlements included Canterbury, Colchester and St Albans. The Trinovantes attacked the Catuvellauni to try to gain Colchester, but the Catuvellauni defeated them and their leader Cunobelinus took over the chieftaincy of both tribes. His authority waned later in his life as dissension grew in his kingdom and when he died it was ruled jointly by his sons Caratacus and Togodumnus.

Before Caratacus and Togodumnus had established a union of the tribal kingdom, a Roman army of about 40,000 arrived on the shores of Kent in AD43, sent by the Emperor Claudius and commanded by Aulus Plautius. Claudius himself arrived to lead his troops into battle against a British force led by Caratacus in a two-day battle at the River Medway in Kent. Eleven British tribes surrendered within 16 days, after which Claudius returned to Rome, leaving Britain under the control of its first Roman governor, Aulus Plautius.

The people of northern England, Wales and Scotland resisted the Romans and the Romans built more than a hundred camps and forts in those areas to try to keep the people there in check. They did not manage to conquer Scotland, which they called 'Caledonia', and a later Roman emperor, Hadrian, ordered a wall to be built across the northern boundary of the empire, with 17 forts along its 118-kilometre length.

Britons and Romans

History objectives (Unit 6A)
• To place the Celtic and Roman periods in a chronological framework.
• To select and record information about Celtic and Roman ways of life.
• To make comparisons between these lifestyles.
• About aspects of life in Celtic and Roman life, using a variety of resources.

Resources

• A large, display-sized timeline on which dates have been written for periods the children have studied, and blank pieces of card
• A map of the world
• Pictures, information books and electronic texts about the Britons and the Romans
• Generic sheets 1–3 (pages 21–23)
• Activity sheets 1–3 (pages 24–26)

Starting points: *whole class*

Ask the children to name events or times in history about which they have learned. On pieces of card write headings for the events or periods they name. Help them to find their places on the timeline by asking them if the events were a very long time ago and if each new one they name was before or after others on the timeline. Ask:

• Which happened first?
• Which events happened recently?
• Which ones happened a very long time ago?

Revise or introduce the terms BC (Before Christ) and AD (Anno Domini, 'in the year of the Lord') as used by historians. Explain that the Universal Calendar (the standardised calendar used all over the world) is based on the Christian calendar from which these terms come. Point out that many people now use the terms BCE (Before the Common Era) and CE (Common Era) instead. Tell the children that they are going to learn about the Roman invasions of Britain and the people who already lived there. Help them to locate 55BC on the timeline.

Ask the children about people who have come to Britain from other parts of the world and why they have done so (for example, to have a better life, to find work or to escape from poverty or persecution – see Chapter 1).

Help them to find Italy, Rome and the Mediterranean Sea on a map of the world. Tell them that the Romans had invaded the lands around the Mediterranean Sea, including France, Spain and parts of Africa, and were ruling those lands. The leaders of the Roman Empire at the time were Julius Caesar, Pompey and Crassus. Julius Caesar was in charge in Gaul (France). Ask:

• Why might Julius Caesar have decided to invade Britain?
• What good would it do?
• What might the Romans do once they arrived in Britain?

Use Generic sheet 1 as reference so that the children can see where the different British tribes lived, and give them copies of Generic sheet 2. Show them the picture of the crannog on Generic sheet 1 and tell them that the British often built these dwellings, especially in Scotland. Discuss what might have made Britain seem attractive to the Romans. Draw out the idea of the wealth that the Romans thought could be found in the form of metals and other materials. Point out that sometimes an invasion might be led by an emperor to convince the people that he was a strong leader who should be kept in power. Also discuss the impressions that people form about other people of whom they know very little – they notice, and sometimes exaggerate, the differences between those people and themselves. Discuss the meanings of the words 'arrive', 'conquer', 'invade', 'land', 'remain', 'settle', 'slave', 'stay', 'trade' and 'visit'.

Ask the children if they think the Romans would have had any surprises when they arrived in Britain and saw the people, their homes and settlements, and their weapons. What might have been the same? What might have been different?

Tell the children that they are now going to find out about the home life of British and Roman people.

Group activities

Activity sheet 1
This sheet is for children who can read an illustrated text, using the pictures as clues for the more difficult words, and are learning to use a dictionary or glossary for looking up new words. They have to label pictures of British and Roman houses using the words given.

Activity sheet 2
This sheet is for children who understand the meanings of 'similarity' and 'difference' and can use a limited range of source material to find out about the similarities and differences between groups of people. They have to make notes about the similarities and differences between British and Roman houses, using the pictures as a guide (including Generic sheet 3 on page 23).

Activity sheet 3
This sheet is for children who can use a chart for recording key facts from their reading of information texts and pictures (including Generic sheet 3 on page 23). They have to make notes about the ways in which the Britons and Romans cooked, kept clean and so on, and compare British and Roman home life.

Plenary session

Invite some of the children who completed Activity sheet 1 to say how British and Roman homes were different from our homes today. Ask them to explain some of the new words they have learned for items in British and Roman homes.

Ask those who completed Activity sheet 2 about the similarities between the houses of the Britons and the Romans. Emphasise that the two cultures had many similarities. Some of the homes that the rich Romans built in Britain have survived and so we know more about them than we do about the poorer homes, which are less likely to have survived because they were made of less durable materials. Emphasise that the poorer Romans had homes with earthen floors covered with rushes or rush mats, and that it was only the rich who had large villas with mosaic floors.
Invite some of the children who completed Activity

sheet 3 to share their discoveries. Discuss what the Britons might have thought of the new houses the Romans built in their country and how they might have viewed the Romans. Also discuss what the Romans might have thought of the Britons.

Ideas for support

Make a pictorial word bank to which the children can refer. Some children could copy or trace pictures of items from British and Roman houses, glue them into a collaborative 'Britons and Romans' glossary (with the pages already headed with the letters A to Z) and label them.

Ideas for extension

On a large piece of paper write the word 'How?' Ask groups of children to find out about a particular aspect of British and Roman life. For example:

- How did they keep clean?
- How did they cook?
- How did they entertain themselves?
- How did they worship?
- How did they build their houses?
- How did they light and heat their houses?
- How did they fight?

Show the children how to use the indexes of books or the opening pages of websites to look for key words that will direct them to answers.

Ask the children to find out about the religions of the Britons and the Romans and to say how we know about them. They could look for similarities and differences between them – for example, both had several gods and goddesses and sometimes made images of them. They had special places which they used for worship, although the Romans had larger, stone buildings.

Ask the children to compile electronic databases about the Britons and the Romans. Help them to make an index and contents or opening page, which others can use to locate information.

Linked ICT activities

Ask the children to search for information about Roman mosaics. They can use CD-Roms, but check with your LEA guidelines on children using search engines (some LEAs provide them for schools) before asking the children to search the internet for information. Tell them that mosaics were made with small coloured tiles, usually forming a picture. Show them some modern tiles (a DIY store will often give you single or cracked tiles) and explain that modern tiling is usually a repeat pattern rather than making a picture.

Tell the children that they are going to produce a design for a tile, using a graphics program on the computer. Give them a 10cm by 10cm square of paper to draw their design on before using the computer.

Using *Dazzle* or Microsoft *Paintbrush* (see Useful resources on pages 126 and 127), let them start by drawing a small tile using the square tool. Let them choose the size of this first tile. When they have drawn the design on the tile, save and print the image.

Show the children how to copy and paste the tile to fill a page. Save the page and print it. Make a display of the single tiles and the whole pages, alongside the original designs and any written descriptions the children want to make.

Britons and Romans

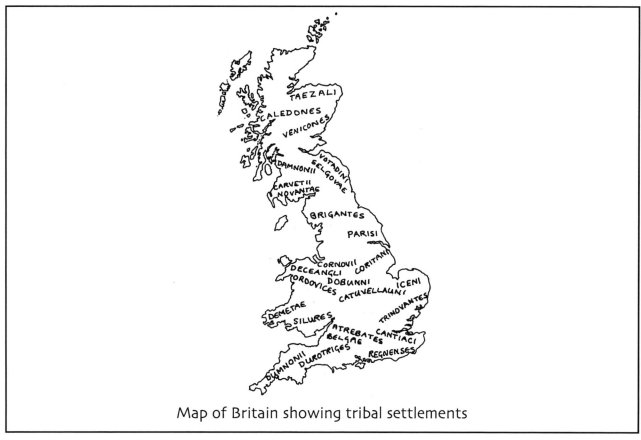

Map of Britain showing tribal settlements

A crannog in Scotland

Britons and Romans

I have conquered Gaul. Britain is not far away. If I invade Britain I need not go back to Rome yet. I could go back even more of a hero if I capture Britain.

The Roman general Julius Caesar

This is my chance to make my name as a great emperor.

The Roman Emperor Claudius

They say that Britain has great wealth. The people there mine metals such as gold, iron and tin. They make wonderful jewellery and weapons with them. There are even pearls found in the oysters there.

Britain is damp and misty but never very cold, and most crops can be grown there apart from grapes and olives. The people grow great quantities of grain.

The Roman historian Tacitus

The forests have no wild beasts or poisonous snakes. The country is full of cows with plenty of milk.

A Roman writer

The people there are savages. They wear hardly any clothes. Their warriors fight naked, their bodies painted with a blue dye and their hair plastered with lime and shaped into spikes. They do this to make themselves look warlike.

A Roman historian

The Britons are made up of many tribes, who are always fighting one another. They will never unite against an invading force.

A Roman soldier

PHOTOCOPIABLE

Britons and Romans

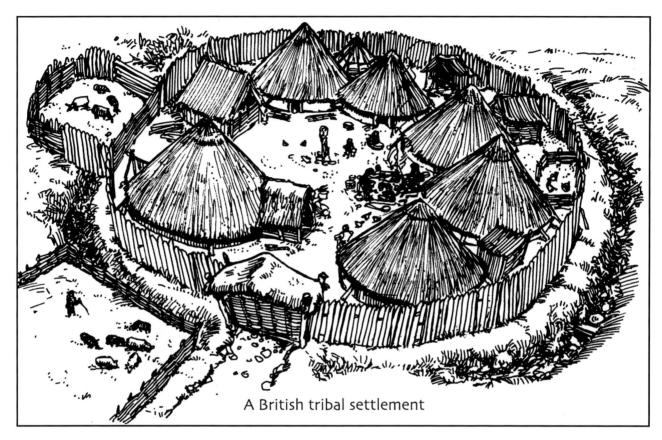

A British tribal settlement

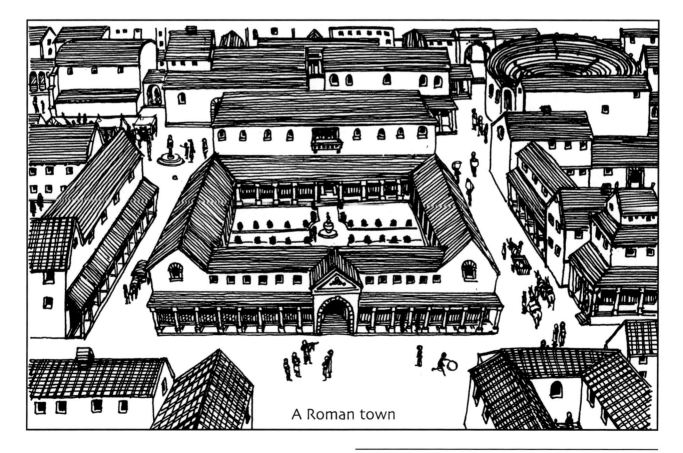

A Roman town

Name _____

Britons and Romans

Use the following words to label the British and Roman houses.

WORD BANK

amphora (made from clay) for wine
clay bowl
clay oil lamp
clay plate
clay pot
couch

earthen floor
fire for heating the house and cooking
iron cooking pot
iron firedogs
stone floor
weaving loom

window
wooden bench
wooden bucket
wooden plate
wooden table

A British house

A Roman house

Name _____

Britons and Romans

A British house

A Roman house

Look for the similarities and differences between the British and Roman houses, and record them in the table below. You could also use Generic sheet 3 to help you.

Similarities	Differences

Name _____

Britons and Romans

Use information texts and pictures to find out about British and Roman life when the Romans first came to Britain. Make notes about what you find out in the table below.

	British life	Roman life
Cooking		
Eating		
Sleeping		
Heating and lighting their homes		
Clothes and hairstyles		
Keeping clean and tidy		

Boudica

CHAPTER 3

TEACHERS' NOTES

Boudica and the Iceni

Boudica (also spelled 'Boudicca' and 'Boadicea'), which is thought to be from the Celtic word for 'victory', was born in about AD25. She was a member of the royal family of the Iceni tribe, which occupied the area now mainly covered by East Anglia (see map on Generic sheet 1, page 31). Much of the information we have about Boudica and her revolt against the Romans comes from accounts written by the Roman historians Tacitus and Dio Cassius. We know the names of some of the kings of the Iceni from their gold and silver coins, many of which can be seen in the British Museum. Many historians think that Prasutagus, the king whom the Romans killed in AD60, was married to Boudica and that they had two daughters named Camorra and Tasca. However, some numismatists believe that the inscriptions on silver coins found in East Anglia have been misinterpreted and that the person named on them was Esuprastus, whom they do not link with Boudica.

Some of the British tribes, notably the Trinovantes, Catuvellauni and Iceni, had made treaties with the Romans. According to Tacitus, Prasutagus had made a will naming the Roman emperor Nero joint heir of his kingdom with his two daughters. However, the Romans treated the Iceni as a defeated nation and forced them to surrender. This meant that young Iceni men were obliged to serve in the Roman army.

The Romans took over the estates of wealthy Iceni and pillaged the countryside, flogged Boudica and raped her daughters. The Roman procurator Catus Decianus claimed that the money and property which the late emperor Claudius had given to members of the tribe had, in fact, been a loan, and claimed it back.

At about the same time the Trinovantes also felt that they were being treated unfairly. Their centre was Colchester, where the Romans had set up a colonia (a settlement for retired legionaries), which they named Camulodunum. Land which the Trinovantes had regarded as theirs had been given

to the retired Roman legionaries, who began to seize even more. The Romans had begun to revere the late emperor Claudius as a god and had built a huge temple in his honour in Colchester. Its remains can be seen in the basement of Castle Museum in Colchester.

In AD60 Boudica called a meeting of the Iceni and Trinovantes at Thetford in Norfolk and urged them to join her in a revolt against the Romans. The first town they would attack was Colchester. The Roman historian Dio Cassius described her as follows:

> 'She was huge of frame, terrifying of aspect, and with a harsh voice. A great mass of bright red hair fell to her knees: she wore a twisted torc, and a tunic of many colours, over which was a thick mantle, fastened by a brooch. Now she grasped a spear, to strike fear into all who watched her.'

Boudica's revolt: Colchester

Boudica led an army of tribespeople to Colchester. The town had no ramparts or ditches and was not well defended because the Roman governor in Britain, Suetonius Paulinus, had taken two legions to Wales to quell unrest there. When the people of Colchester heard that the rebels were on their way they appealed to the procurator Catus Decianus for help, but he could spare only 200 men (and they were not well armed). A Roman commander from the East Midlands heard of Colchester's plight, and led his legion south to rescue them, but the Britons ambushed him, and his army of about 1,500 infantry was wiped out. He fled to the fort at Longthorpe in Peterborough with his cavalry. Excavations have revealed another hastily built smaller fort there, which could be defended by fewer people.

Boudica's army charged into Colchester and set fire to the Temple of Claudius in which most of the Romans had taken refuge. They looted the city and destroyed Roman statues and tombstones. The famous bronze head from a statue of Claudius was found in the River Alde in Suffolk – the head had clearly been wrenched from the body. Archaeologists have found tombstones showing signs of deliberate destruction and with very little erosion by weathering, notably the tombstone of Longinus (see opposite).

The excavations of archaeologists support the (Roman) written accounts of Boudica's rebellion – they revealed a layer of burnt debris beneath the modern city of Colchester, across the parts which were occupied in AD60.

Boudica's revolt: London

As at Colchester, the Britons killed everyone in London (Londinium) and looted and burned the buildings. Archaeologists have found a burnt layer beneath London, too. Suetonius Paulinus had heard that Boudica's army was on its way to London, but had decided that he must abandon London and wait for all of his army to march from Wales. So London, like Colchester, was not defended. Boudica's army moved north along Watling Street (a major Roman road) to St Albans (Verulamium) and set fire to it. As in Colchester and London, a burnt layer has been found during excavations. However, in St Albans there was not total destruction; several buildings remained standing. Unlike at Colchester and London, no collections of burnt grain or parcels of coins have been found. Historians think this suggests that people there might have had time to escape with some of their possessions. After this, the Romans took action to stop Boudica's army.

Boudica's last battle

Paulinus gathered an army (some sources say it consisted of 10,000 men) and chose the site of the battle against Boudica's host of tribespeople. The Romans took up a position in a narrow valley facing an open plain (somewhere along Watling Street – the exact location is unknown). A thick wood protected their rear. The Britons massed on the plain, some on foot, some on horseback and others in horse-drawn chariots. According to Dio Cassius, there were 230,000 of them. Their families lined the battlefield in carts and on foot to watch their expected victory. As the Britons charged to attack the Romans, they were funnelled into a narrow area. The Roman infantry launched their javelins and then advanced in wedge formation. The Roman cavalry shot forward and the Britons turned and fled, but their many carts and chariots impeded their escape. Large numbers of them, including women, were killed by the Romans.

The tombstone of Longinus, depicting a Roman cavalryman whose horse is stepping over a naked, cowering Briton. The stone had been smashed into six pieces and lay face down in the earth; the face had been hacked off and was found only in 1996 in a garden. The tombstone is in Castle Museum, Colchester.

Some say that after the defeat, Boudica killed herself by taking poison. Others argue that she had no reason to do that – she could have gathered more forces and fought on, and there was no shame in losing this battle. It is suggested that she actually died from an illness.

Boudica

LESSON PLAN

History objectives (Unit 6A)
- To explore in detail the reasons for Boudica's revolt and its consequences.
- That sources about Boudica contradict each other.
- That there are different opinions about Boudica.

Resources

- Several pictures of Boudica such as the statue by Thomas Thornycroft (1902) on the Embankment in London, the sculpture by J Howard Thomas (1915) in Cardiff Museum, and the stained glass window (1902) in Colchester Museum
- Generic sheets 1–3 (pages 31–33)
- Activity sheets 1–3 (pages 34–36)

Starting points: *whole class*

Tell the children that Boudica was born in about AD25. Show them pictures of her and point out the dates when the paintings or sculptures were made. What can the children find out about Boudica from the pictures? Ask:

- What does she look like?
- What is she wearing?
- What kind of weapons did she have?
- What kind of transport did she use?
- Who is with her in the pictures?

Ask the children to compare the appearance of Boudica in the different pictures, noting any similarities and differences. Read out the description of her written at the time by the Roman historian Dio Cassius:

> 'She was huge of frame, terrifying of aspect, and with a harsh voice. A great mass of bright red hair fell to her knees: she wore a twisted torc, and a tunic of many colours, over which was a thick mantle, fastened by a brooch. Now she grasped a spear, to strike fear into all who watched her.'

Explain what a torc and a mantle are (see Glossary on page 121). Can the children see them in the pictures? Compare the description with the pictures.

Point out that Boudica and most of her people did not wear armour, although some of them wore helmets and carried shields. Their weapons were simple spears, sticks, stones and swords. The children might notice the blades attached to the wheels of Boudica's chariot. Tell them that the chariots of the time did not have blades on the wheels, but artists tended to add them.

Show the children the map of Roman Britain (Generic sheet 1), showing the areas occupied by the British tribes, and point out the lands of the Iceni, Boudica's tribe. Tell them about the events leading up to Boudica's revolt and about the attacks on Colchester, London and St Albans, drawing attention to how the Britons succeeded in those attacks. (They took the Roman settlements by surprise, and there were few soldiers there to defend their settlements.)

Give the children copies of Generic sheet 2 and read the text in the first two paragraphs while they follow it. Ask them who they think has the better chance of winning the battle. Note the numbers in each army and tell them about each side's weapons and any armour. Also tell them that Suetonius Paulinus was an experienced general in the Roman army. He knew that the Britons would have a better chance if they were allowed to spring surprise attacks. Tell them that the Roman army was well trained, whereas the British army came from two different tribes and had no organised training.

Read on with the children and discuss the speeches made by Suetonius Paulinus and Boudica to their troops. Ask the children to explain why they made these speeches. After reading the story, ask the children to explain how the Romans managed to defeat an army that was eight times as large as their own. Point out the superior tactics of Suetonius Paulinus, the training and discipline of the Roman army, and their superior weapons and armour. Also discuss how Boudica had defeated the Romans in Colchester, St Albans and London, noting that in those places the Britons did not fight pitched battles with the Romans in which skill and good organisation were essential.

Tell the children that they are now going to find out more about Boudica.

Group activities

Activity sheet 1

This sheet is for children who can find information from pictures. With help, they can use charts for recording the information they find. They are learning to question historical sources and beginning to realise that different people have different opinions about people in history and that historians interpret information differently. They have to study the two pictures and fill in a chart detailing what they have found out about Boudica from the sources.

Activity sheet 2

This sheet is for children who are developing skills in finding information from written sources and in using charts for recording and organising information. They recognise that different sources can be used to find out different types of information. They can question historical sources and realise that historians interpret information differently. They have to study some quotations and fill in a chart detailing what they have found out about Boudica from the sources.

Activity sheet 3

This sheet is for children who can find information from written sources and can use charts for organising and recording information from different sources. They understand that different people have different views about events in history and that new evidence and new interpretations of evidence can affect historians' views. They need a copy of Generic sheet 3 to complete this activity. They have to study the sources on Generic sheet 3 and fill in the chart. A copy of Generic sheet 2 would also be helpful.

Plenary session

Invite some of the children who completed Activity sheet 1 to read out what the pictures tell them about Boudica. Do the pictures give the same or different impressions of her? In what way? Discuss the facts found from written sources by the children who worked on Activity sheet 2. Ask them who Boudica was and what she was like. Invite some of the children who completed Activity sheet 3 to read out anything their sources tell them that supports what has been said already, plus any evidence that questions it.

Emphasise that as new evidence is found by archaeologists and historians, historians change their views about what happened and what people were like in the past. Also point out that the same evidence can give different ideas to different historians.

Ideas for support

Children who have difficulty in understanding what happened during Boudica's last battle could be helped to enact it using models.

Ideas for extension

Discuss the sources from which we know about Boudica's revolt – for example, the writings of Roman historians and military people and the work of archaeologists. Point out the ways in which recent archaeological work, especially in Colchester and London, has helped historians to check information from other sources, such as writings. Ask the children to research the revolt using a range of sources such as museum exhibits, information books, CD-Roms, Roman remains, and downloaded material from information websites and museum websites.

Linked ICT activities

Ask the children to find out more about the Romans and Boudica. They can use CD-Roms, but check with your LEA guidelines on children using search engines (some LEAs provide them for schools) before asking the children to search the internet for information. An alternative useful starting point is the BBC website (see Useful resources on page 127). Talk to the children about the internet and what it really is (a database of information). Remind them that we don't always know who has put the information on a website, so not all the information they find might be true or reliable. This is why we need to use different sources of information to gather facts.

Using information gathered from a variety of sources, create a class file about Boudica (as a teacher-led activity with the whole class or with groups during the literacy hour). Use a word processing program to create on screen a sheet similar to Activity sheet 3 (see page 36). Ask the children to contribute facts from the activity. As they read these out, either you or one of the children can type them in. The fact file can be saved and printed for use as an information source. Include references to where the facts originated.

Boudica's Britain

Map of Britain showing where the Iceni lived and the positions of Colchester, St Albans and London

Boudica's last battle

In the late summer of AD60 Suetonius Paulinus, the Roman governor of Britain, was in north Wales with an army, trying to capture Anglesey. News came that Boudica, with a horde of Britons, had destroyed Camulodunum (Colchester). He headed south-west with an army of 10 000.

Boudica and her people had also sacked the Roman towns of Londinium (London) and Verulamium (St Albans). There were about 80 000 of them heading north up Watling Street to do battle with Suetonius Paulinus.

Suetonius Paulinus waited for the Britons somewhere along Watling Street. There was a wood behind him and open ground in front, from where the Britons would come. He said:

> Ignore the noise of the Britons! Most of them are women, with no weapons, who cannot fight!

Boudica drove her chariot in front of her people and urged them on:

> We have beaten one Roman legion that dared to try and stop us! We are strong enough without armour! They will flee from us in fear!

When they reached the place where the Roman army was, they charged forward.

The Romans marched forward in a wedge shape, aiming their spears. Soon many Britons lay dead. The Romans hit the other Britons with their shields and killed them with their swords.

The Britons could not escape. They were hemmed in by their chariots and horses. Nearly every one of them was killed. Only 400 Romans died.

Boudica escaped, but she died soon afterwards. Historians think she poisoned herself rather than be captured.

Boudica

For use with Activity sheet 3.

A 'This is not the first time Britons have been led into battle by a woman. A Roman legion dared to face the warlike Britons: they paid for it with their lives. Those who survived think only about running away as cowards. The Romans shrink with terror from the shouts of the British army. What will they be like when the battle begins? Look around at your numbers, at the proud display of warlike spirits, and think about why we draw our swords. We must either conquer or die with glory. Though a woman, my resolution is fixed: the men, if they like, may survive as cowards, and live in captivity.'

Tacitus, a Roman historian, quoting Boudica

B Boudica was married to Prasutagus, the king of the Iceni tribe in East Anglia. They had two daughters. Prasutagus was a weak king, who did not want a war. So he made a pact with the Romans saying that all his lands and riches would be split between his daughters and the Romans when he died.

A twentieth-century school textbook

C Archaeologists in Colchester found that when Boudica's troops seized the city they destroyed anything touched by the Romans. Many of the houses were built of hardened clay and timber, and would have been very difficult to burn. But every house had been completely flattened.

A twentieth-century newspaper report

D Boudica sacrificed enemies she defeated in battle to the goddess Andrasta. She took no captives. So Boudica might not have been her real name, but an official title. That would mean that her followers thought of her as the human form of a goddess, or maybe she was a priestess. Perhaps that was why they let a woman lead them into battle.

A twentieth-century historian

Boudica

E British women are nearly as tall as the men, whom they rival in courage. They fight alongside the men, and are just as strong.

Diodorus Siculus, a Roman

F The idea that Prasutagus was the name of Boudica's husband came from Iron Age silver coins found in East Anglia, showing that there was an important person of that name. But some coin experts think this might be wrong. The name on the coins might be something else (Esuprastus). We can no longer be sure that Prasutagus was the name of a king of the Iceni or Boudica's husband.

A twentieth-century television programme

Name _____

Boudica

What can you find out about Boudica from the pictures?
Fill in the table below.

	Source A	Source B
Boudica's family		
What she looked like		
Her clothes and jewellery		
Her weapons		
The transport she used		
Her character		

PHOTOCOPIABLE

Name _____

Boudica

What can you find out about Boudica from the quotations?
Fill in the table below.

To us Romans, Boudica is a killer queen and we use her name to frighten children. In Londinium you can see the marks where her troops burned the buildings. People still find the bones of the people who tried to escape from the bloodthirsty Iceni.

A Roman woman in London

British women are nearly as tall as the men, whom they rival in courage. They fight alongside the men, and are just as strong.

The Roman writer Diodorus Siculus

The Roman writer Dio Cassius

She was very tall. Her eyes seemed to stab you. Her voice was harsh and loud. Her thick, reddish-brown hair hung down below her waist. She always wore a great golden torc around her neck and a flowing tartan mantle fastened with a brooch.

Boudica was married to Prasutagus, the king of the Iceni tribe in East Anglia. They had two daughters. Prasutagus was a weak king, who did not want a war. So he made a pact with the Romans saying that all his lands and riches would be split between his daughters and the Romans when he died.

A twentieth-century British writer

	Facts	Sources
Boudica's family		
What she looked like		
Her clothes and jewellery		
The transport she used		
Her character		

Boudica

What can you find out about Boudica from Sources A to F on Generic sheet 3?
Complete the table. Use Generic sheet 2 to help you.

	Information	Source
Boudica's family		
What she looked like		
Her clothes and jewellery		
Her weapons		
Her character		
Her religion		
What the Britons thought of her		
What the Romans thought of her		

Roman Britain

TEACHERS' NOTES

The Roman occupation of Britain ended between AD400 and 410, when the last legions left, but the Romans left many long-term and even permanent reminders of their presence.

Settlements

Many Romano-British settlements grew up around Roman auxiliary forts. Tradespeople were attracted to the areas by the potential customers – soldiers with regular salaries. The Ordnance Survey splits the settlements of Roman Britain into different types, explained on Generic sheet 1 (see page 42).

Roads

Roman surveyors planned the routes of their roads. Engineers cleared the ground and laid foundations of clay, chalk or gravel, and then laid cement and paving stones on top. The roads linked their settlements and forts both to aid trade and to transport soldiers and military equipment. The roads were straight where possible, but on steep slopes they zigzagged up the slope to facilitate travelling. See the map of Roman roads on Generic sheet 2 (see page 43).

Hadrian's Wall

In AD122, after his imperial tour of inspection in Britain, Emperor Hadrian ordered the construction of the wall and fortifications known as 'Hadrian's Wall'. It stretched 118 kilometres from the Solway Firth, near Carlisle, on the west coast, to Wallsend (near Newcastle upon Tyne) on the east coast. It is about two to four metres wide and five to seven metres high with a ditch three metres deep and nine metres wide on the northern side and a flat bottomed ditch on the southern side. The wall is made of local materials – mainly stone in the east and turf in the west.

There were fortresses at various points along it and fortified gateways called 'milecastles' at intervals of about 1,480 metres. The wall was intended to mark the northernmost frontier of the area of Britain that the Romans were able to govern and to control; it was not intended to prevent movement across this border. At the milecastles, tolls were imposed on goods carried from one side to the other, thus

raising money for the Roman administration. Fragments have survived of some of the wafer-thin postcard-sized wooden tablets on which transactions were recorded. Many of the soldiers on duty along the wall were not Romans but Dutch and Belgian.

The Antonine Wall

Construction of the Antonine Wall was begun in AD142, during the reign of Emperor Antoninus Pius, when the Romans wanted to push the northern boundary of Britannia northwards into Caledonia (Scotland). The Antonine Wall was about 60 kilometres long, stretching from Bridgeness on the River Forth in the east, to Old Kilpatrick on the River Clyde in the west. It was a rampart of soil covered with turf and resting on a foundation of stone, whereas Hadrian's Wall was built mainly of stone. It was originally just over three and a half metres high, and on the north side there was a V-shaped ditch just over twelve metres wide and three and a half metres deep. To the south of the wall there was a cobbled road (called the 'Military Way') which linked the forts along the wall every two miles. These forts were barracks for soldiers who were sent to defend the northern frontier of Britannia.

Roman sites

Remains of the following structures can be found at excavated Roman settlements and forts.

Houses
Excavation of a villa which belonged to a wealthy Roman or Romano-British family, or an important Roman such as the commanding officer of a garrison, might reveal some of the following: kitchens with stone ovens built into the walls, servants' quarters and storerooms, a hypocaust for heating (see page 38), and a shrine in which statuettes of the household gods (the lares and penates) were kept.

Plumbing
The Romans built plumbing systems to supply drinking water and water for bathhouses, and for drains. They used clay pipes and stone drains. Only

the wealthiest Romans had running water and their own lavatories in their houses. Most people had to fetch water (or send a slave to fetch it) from a well or spring.

Latrines

At public bathhouses in several towns and at forts such as Housesteads and Vindolanda near Hadrian's Wall, excavators have uncovered the remains of public latrines. The stone latrines had drains beneath them and traces of wood show that they had wooden seats. Like other public latrines, water (often diverted from a stream) ran constantly along channels. There were no private cubicles; it was a communal area seating several people (at Vindolanda the public latrine had seats for 16 people). Remnants of sponges attached to sticks have been found, which were used as toilet paper; they were washed in a channel of running water.

Bathhouses

Public bathhouses were a feature of Roman towns. As well as having a practical function they were social meeting places, where people met to chat, relax and play board games and dice. They had several rooms, each with a special purpose in the bathing process. The bath at Vindolanda was lined with clay tiles: some complete tiles as well as many fragments have been found there. The walls of bathhouses were often plastered and decorated with painted pictures or patterns.

Hypocausts

Examples of this form of central heating system can be seen at several excavated Roman sites. The stone floors of the rooms were supported on pillars. A furnace, which was usually outside the house, had a stokehole through which fuel could be put into the furnace. Hot air from the furnace would flow beneath the floors through ducts into the rooms above. There were flues through which smoke could escape from the furnace. Poorer Roman homes in Britain would not have had this form of heating. They were more likely to have a fire in a stone hearth or, like the Britons, a fire surrounded by stones on the earthen floor of a round hut, with a hole in the roof for smoke to escape. A hypocaust was used to heat the water and the warm rooms at public bathhouses.

Temples

The Romans built temples to their gods, and incorporated the gods worshipped in Britain and in other lands in their empire into their worship. They often built shrines to local gods in order to placate them or ask for their blessing. These shrines would often be near a well or spring, and excavations have revealed many items that must have been left there as offerings: amulets and charms, cheaply made clay figurines (made specially for the purpose of religious offerings), animal bones and even human skulls.

Amphitheatres

Outside the walls of most Roman settlements there was an amphitheatre in which free public entertainment took place: animal-baiting, gladiatorial combats, wild beast hunts and wrestling. The amphitheatre was usually an oval or circular arena with tiered seating around it. The remains of a large amphitheatre can be seen at Chester, for instance.

Writing

The Romans brought not only the Latin language to Britain, but also a writing system. The Britons had no written form for their language (so there are no written British sources from which we can find out about life at the time, only Roman ones). As well as carved writing on stone, of which many examples can be found, the Romans wrote with ink on both wood and parchment. Examples of their pens and inkwells can be seen in museums such as the Museum of London (see Useful resources on page 125). They also had notebooks for temporary writing; they consisted of wooden writing tablets on which a layer of beeswax was spread. A stylus was used for writing on the wax; the writing could be erased using the flat end of the stylus. See Generic sheet 2 on page 43, and Generic sheet 3 on page 44 for numerals.

Walls

Walls were constructed of stone and mortar and were built both to defend a settlement and to control the movement of people and goods in and out of it. The remains of town walls can be seen in settlements such as London, St Albans, Chester, Lincoln and York. In some of these sites the entrance gateways can still be seen. Note that 'gate' (as in Coppergate in York, Aldgate in London and Northgate in Chester) does not, in fact, mean 'gate' but 'street'; it comes from *gata* (Old Norse, street).

Roman Britain

LESSON PLAN

History objectives (Unit 6A)
- About evidence that tells us about life in Roman Britain.
- Ask and answer questions about what survived from the Roman settlement of Britain.

Resources

- A large outline map of Britain in the form of a tracing or an OHT on which roads and settlements can be marked
- Pictures and information about major Roman settlements in Britain and any Roman sites in the school's locality
- Pictures of inscriptions of Roman numerals and Latin inscriptions (for example, clocks, tombs and monuments)
- A calendar
- Generic sheets 1–4 (pages 42–45)
- Activity sheets 1–3 (pages 46–48)

Starting points: *whole class*

Show the children a map of Britain and help them to find the area where they live. Tell them about some of the places where the Romans built towns or fortifications and mark these places on the map. Include significant Roman settlements and structures such as London, St Albans, Colchester, Chester, Silchester, Hadrian's Wall and any others in the local area. (Show the extent of the Roman settlements by sharing the map on Generic sheet 2.) Show the children pictures of some of the remains which have been uncovered in these places, such as town walls, bathhouses, villas, amphitheatres, forums and basilicas.

Explain that these remains have helped us to understand how the Romans lived all those years ago in Britain. Tell them that some of the Celts at that time liked the Roman way of life so much that they copied some of their ways. Tell them that they built villas and adapted Roman clothing and pottery styles, for example.

Tell the children that some of the Roman ways of life are still used in Britain today. Show the children a calendar and tell them that the names of the months come from the Roman calendar. Some of the months in our calendar were named after Roman gods – for example, January (Janus), February (Februus), March (Mars), April (Aprilis), May (Maia), June (Juno). July and August were named after Julius Caesar and Augustus Caesar. The others were named because of their position in the Roman calendar – September (seventh month), October (eighth month), November (ninth month) and December (tenth month). The Roman calendar had 10 months in a year of 304 days: Martius, Aprilis, Maius, Junius, Quintilis, Sextilis, September, October, November, December. The names of some of the days of the week are based on their Roman origins – Saturday (dies Saturni, Saturn's day), Sunday (dies solis, sun's day), Monday (dies lunae, moon's day).

Explain that another Roman influence still used today is Roman numerals – for example, on clock faces and sundials, monuments, cinema film release dates, tombs and inscriptions. Explain how the numbers are written, using Generic sheet 3.

Tell the children that they are now going to look at one aspect of Roman life in more detail. Give the children copies of Generic sheet 4. Tell them that the pictures and information are based on what has been found at a Roman site in Britain. Tell them that the Roman philosopher Seneca lived close to a bathhouse in Rome. He wrote a letter complaining about the noise – for example, 'the man who likes to sing in the bath; men who jump into the water with an almighty splash; and then the cries of "Cakes for sale" and "Hot sausages".' Ask them what this tells us about the activities at the bathhouse. Was it just a place where people went to wash themselves?

Ask the children what kind of modern building the bathhouse reminds them of and discuss what they can find out about the bathhouse from the evidence in the picture and text. What can they find out about how people used the bathhouse and the things they used for washing?

Tell the children they are now going to use sources to find some more information about life in Roman Britain.

Group activities

Activity sheet 1

This sheet is for children who are learning how to use a limited range of historical artefacts (or pictures of them) to find out about the lives of people in the past. They know that the Romans came and settled in Britain a very long time ago and that some of the things they made, built and wrote have survived. They are learning to select sources to find the answers to questions. They are required to decide which pictures answer which questions about Roman remains and then ask their own question about an amphitheatre.

Activity sheet 2

This sheet is for children who can select from a limited range of sources to find the answers to questions about the lives of people in the past. They know that the Romans came and colonised Britain some 2,000 years ago and can talk about some of the things they made, built and wrote which have survived. They have to decide which picture answers which question about Roman remains and write a one-sentence answer for each one. They are then required to write their own question and use reference sources to draw a picture relating to it.

Activity sheet 3

This sheet is for children who can look for sources to find the answers to questions about the lives of people in the past. They can select the sources that they think are most likely to provide answers to questions and make notes to help them to write answers to those questions. They know that the Romans came and colonised Britain some 2,000 years ago and can name and talk about some of the things they made, built and wrote which have survived. They have to answer some questions about Roman remains as well as pose one of their own, deciding which sources to use to locate the answers.

Plenary session

Invite some of the children who completed Activity sheets 1 and 2 to say what they think they can find out by looking at the pictures. Ask some of those who completed Activity sheet 2 to read the sentences they have written in answer to each question and to say which picture helped them. Invite some of the children who completed Activity sheet 3 to read out their own question and answer. Ask all the groups to say what sources they found most helpful in answering their questions. How did they know which sources would help them and what did they find out? Encourage them to refer to their notes while giving their answers.

Discuss the new words (and their meanings) which the children have learned for Roman artefacts: amphitheatre, hypocaust, Latin, mosaic, stylus, tabula. Ask the children how the Romans changed life in Britain and how they think looking at Roman remains has helped us to understand more about the past.

Ideas for support

With the children working on Activity sheets 1 and 2, discuss the pictures in detail together, reminding the children that some are pictures of remains - not how they would have looked in Roman times. Encourage them to ask questions in order to elicit what they may have been used for, what they may have been made from, why they think they have survived until today and so on.

With the children working on Activity sheet 3, model how to decide which reference sources about Roman remains will give useful information to answer the questions. Show the children how to make notes about the key features.

Ideas for extension

Ask the children what else they would like to find out about life in Roman Britain. Write up their questions and ask them which can be answered by looking at things the Romans left behind.

Plan a visit to a Roman site. Tell the children about the types of things they will see there: the remains of buildings and roads, artefacts, reconstructions, artists' impressions based on the remains and writings and patterns or pictures from the time. Show the children some unlabelled pictures of the types of remains which can be seen at the site, and ask them what they think the things are and what we can learn from them. Discuss how archaeologists and historians can help us to learn from what can be seen by pointing out and explaining key features and by reconstructing things.

Linked ICT activities

Discuss with the children what life might have been like before people started to use writing. Talk about the different ways we use writing today (pen and paper, word processor, email, text messages).

Remind them what a stylus is and show a collection of different writing tools used today (pencils, crayons, cartridge pens). Talk about when we use these tools. Would you use a crayon in an exercise book?

Look at different examples of Roman script and numerals from the pictures of inscriptions used in the lesson. How are these the same as or different from the numbers and text we use today? Using a word processing program, look at different fonts.

Look for fonts similar in style to the letters used by the Romans (such as Times, Trajan, Baskerville). Compare these to the fonts we see used for headings or headlines in books and newspapers (such as Arial, Helvetica, Sassoon).

Ask the children to choose the name of a provincial capital, colony or tribal capital in Roman Britain (see Generic sheet 1). They should write it in a font similar in style to the way the Romans would have written it. Ask them to increase the font size to make the word as large as possible, and print it. Then they should choose a modern font and write the modern name for the place, enlarging and printing the results. Make a class display from the names.

Roman Britain

Roman settlements

Provincial capital
Londinium (London) became established as the Roman capital in Britain (Britannia), a centre of commerce and administration for the Roman province in Britain. The first Roman capital in Britain had been Colchester, but the Romans found London a more convenient location.

Colonies (coloniae)
These were planned settlements for retired veteran soldiers. After ending their service with the army, through old age, injury or illness, they became citizens of Rome. There were four Roman coloniae in Britain:

Camulodunum (Colchester, Essex)   Lindum (Lincoln)

Glevum (Gloucester)   Eboracum (York)

Tribal capitals (civitates)
These were the Roman local government centres for the British tribal regions. They each had a council made up of chieftains and landowners who kept law and order and collected taxes. Through this system the Romans gained the loyalty of many British tribal leaders, who found it best to keep peace with the Romans. There were at least 15 of these tribal capitals, each of which had a Roman name, usually combined with a Romanised form of the tribal name:

Calleva Atrebatum (Silchester, Hampshire)   Corinium Dobunorum (Cirencester, Gloucestershire)
Durnovaria (Dorchester, Dorset)   Durovernum Cantiacorum (Canterbury, Kent)
Isca Dumnoniorum (Exeter, Devon)   Isurium Brigantum (Aldborough, North Yorkshire)
Maridunum (Carmarthen, Dyfed)   Noviomagus Regnensium (Chichester, Sussex)
Petuaria (Brough on Humber, Humberside)   Venta Belgarum (Winchester, Hampshire)   Venta
Icenorum (Caistor St Edmund, Norfolk)   Viroconium Cornoviorum (Wroxeter, Shropshire)
Venta Silurum (Caerwent, Gwent)   Verulamium (St Albans, Hertfordshire)
Ratae Coritanorum (Leicester)

Spa towns
These were built around naturally occurring springs:

Aquae Arnemetiae (Buxton, Derbyshire)   Aquae Sulis (Bath)

Vici
These were small settlements which developed along streets which led from the main gate of the fort. If a fort was used for a long enough time a vicus grew into a town. The industries and trade which followed brought wealth (and more people) into the area, and this, in turn, attracted more civilians to settle there. The governing bodies of a resulting town would be able to raise funds to build a forum (marketplace), a basilica (local government centre) and a temple, as well as buildings designed for public amenities, such as a bathhouse and an amphitheatre. There were also large settlements or towns and various types of fort, some of which grew into larger settlements.

PHOTOCOPIABLE

Roman Britain

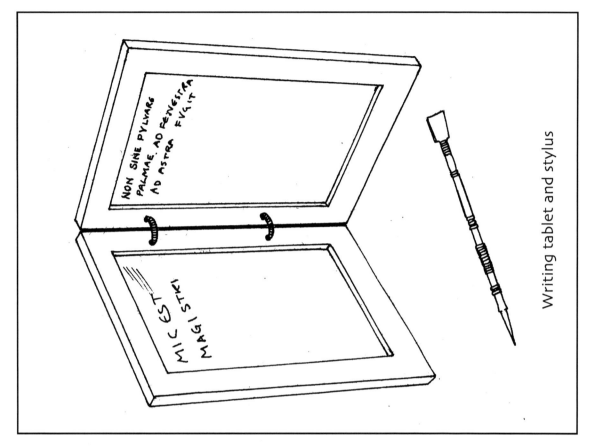

NON SINE PVLVARS
PALMAE. AD PENESTRA
AD ASTRA EVGIT

MIC EST
MAGISTRI

Writing tablet and stylus

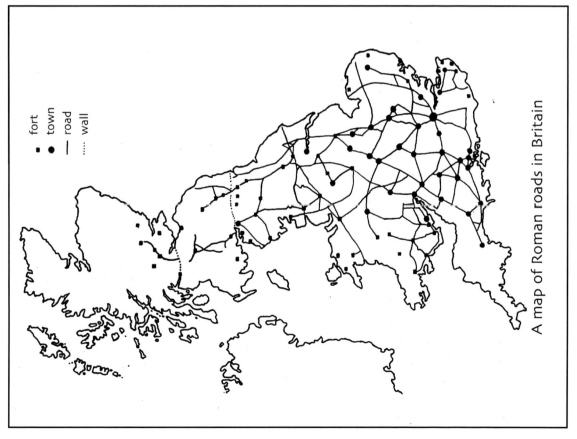

■ fort
● town
— road
····· wall

A map of Roman roads in Britain

Roman Britain

Numbers

Roman numerals are still used on many memorials as well as on some clocks and watches.

Arabic	Roman	Latin word	Arabic	Roman	Latin word
1	I	unus	13	XIII	tredecim
2	II	duo	14	XIV	quattuordecim
3	III	tres	15	XV	quindecim
4	IV	quattuor	16	XVI	sedecim
5	V	quinque	17	XVII	septendecim
6	VI	sex	18	XVIII	duodeviginti
7	VII	septem	19	XIX	undeviginti
8	VIII	octo	20	XX	viginti
9	IX	novem	50	L	quinquaginta
10	X	decem	100	C	centum
11	XI	undecim	500	D	quingenti
12	XII	duodecim	1000	M	mille

You can work out the written forms of other numbers from the following pattern:

IV	=	4	(one before five)
VI	=	6	(one after five)
IX	=	9	(one before ten)
XI	=	11	(one after ten)
XXX	=	30	(three tens)
XL	=	40	(ten before fifty)
XLIV	=	44	(ten before fifty + one before five)
CD	=	400	(one hundred before five hundred)
CCXLVIII = CC+XL+V+III = 248			(two hundreds (200) + ten before fifty (40) + five + three (8))
CDXXIX = CD+XX+IX = 429			(one hundred before five hundred (400) + two tens (20) + one before ten (9))
MCDLXXIV =M+CD+L+XX+IV = 1474			(one thousand (1000) + one hundred before five hundred (400) + fifty + two tens (70) + one before five (4))

Roman Britain

A Roman bathhouse

The remains of bathhouses have been found at many Roman settlements and forts in Britain. This one is at Bearsden in Glasgow, which was a fort near the western end of the Antonine Wall.

At the entrance people paid a small fee to go into the baths. They would go into the apodyterium (changing room). There were niches where they left their clothes. In larger bathhouses there would be a gymnasium where people could exercise.

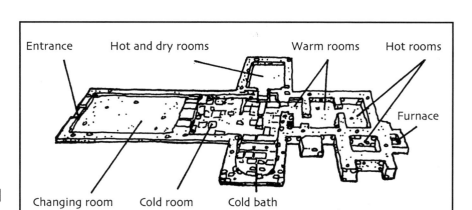

A plan of the bathhouse at Bearsden

After having their bodies cleaned with oils, the bathers would go into the tepidaria (warm rooms) where they could bathe, with other people, in a large warm bath. There were also hot rooms, including a very hot dry room called a caldarium or tepidarium, and a laconium or sudatorium (sweat room) where they could relax.

Before leaving the bathhouse the bathers would take a cold dip in the frigidarium (cold room).

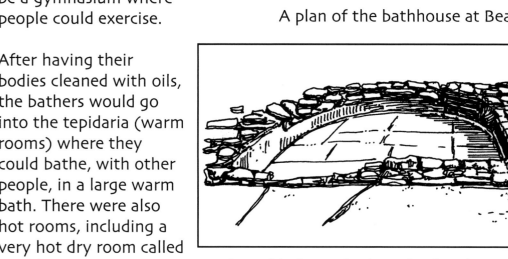

The cold plunge bath in the frigidarium at Bearsden

After exercising, people would rub their bodies with oils (or pay a slave to do this for them) and then scrape off the oil, dirt and sweat with a scraper called a strygil.

An oil flask and a strygil

Name _____

Roman Britain

Which pictures will help to answer the questions? Write the correct numbers in the boxes.

How did rich Romans decorate their houses? □

What were Roman roads like? □

How did the Romans write? □

1 road

2 tabula and stylus

3 mosaic floor

Look at the picture below. Read the sentences.

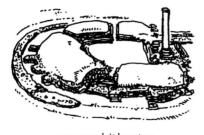

an amphitheatre

This is a picture of the remains of an amphitheatre. It was where Romans went to watch entertainment such as wrestling and animal-baiting. The four mounds on the outside of the picture are where the seating would have been.

Write a question about something you want to find out about the amphitheatre.

_____

_____

Name _____

Roman Britain

Which pictures help to answer the five questions below? Write the number of the picture in the box; then write a sentence to answer the question. Use books and CD-Roms to help you.

Now write a question of your own and draw a picture in box 6 to match it.

How did rich Romans heat their houses?	
What were Roman roads like?	
How did the Romans write?	
How did rich Romans decorate their houses?	
Where did the Romans go for entertainment?	
	6

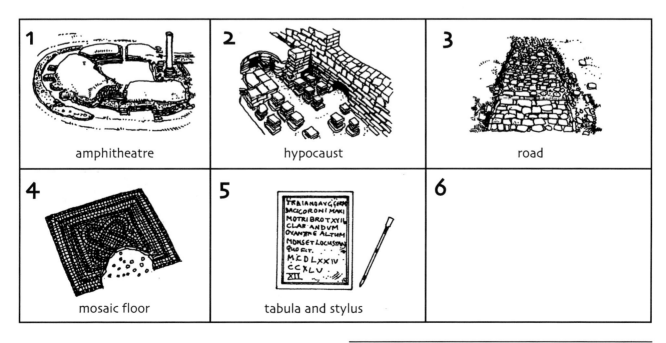

1 amphitheatre

2 hypocaust

3 road

4 mosaic floor

5 tabula and stylus

6

Name _____

Roman Britain

Find out the answers to these questions. Complete the table.
Then write a question of your own to answer.

Question	Where I found the answer	Answer
How did rich Romans heat their houses?		
What were Roman roads like?		
How did the Romans write?		
How did rich Romans decorate their houses?		
Where did the Romans go for entertainment?		
My question:		

PHOTOCOPIABLE

The Anglo-Saxons

CHAPTER 5

TEACHERS' NOTES

The departure of the Romans and the coming of the Anglo-Saxons

Between AD400 and 410 the Roman legions were withdrawn from Britain. Written records from just before this time include those of the Roman writer Ammianus Marcellinus (c.330–390). His history of the Roman Empire from AD98 to the events of his own lifetime records the Saxons, Picts and Scots as 'barbarians' who were attacking Britain in about 365. He describes gangs of looters surrounding London and driving captured men and cattle along the roads. The emperor Honorius was approached for help against such raiders in 410 but the answer he sent to the Britons was that they should defend themselves. At that time other parts of the Roman Empire were being given priority (for instance, Rome had been attacked by the Goths).

After the Romans left, some towns (such as Exeter) were abandoned. In others the Roman buildings such as marketplaces and bathhouses fell into disrepair. The materials were taken and reused – for example, tiles from bathhouses were used for flooring elsewhere.

By about AD430 a warlord named Vortigern (Vawr Tigherne, 'the Great Leader') was ruling most of Britain. According to Nennius, Vortigern hired Saxon mercenaries to repel attacks from the Picts and Scots. He gave them a patch of land on the Isle of Thanet, Kent, and then stopped paying them. The Saxons were aggrieved and returned to attack the Britons.

The Britons were divided among themselves and not in a strong position to resist attacks from invaders: Saxons from the east as well as raids by the Picts, the Irish and the Scots. The writings of St Gildas (c.493–570) provide evidence that the Britons were having difficulty in defending themselves against the Saxon raiders in the fifth century: he wrote that the Britons sent messages to the Roman consul 'Agitius' (probably Aetius) asking him to send Roman forces to save them from the invaders:

'To Aetius, thrice consul, the groans of the Britons … The barbarians push us to the sea; the sea pushes us back on the barbarians. Between these two kinds of death, we are either drowned or slaughtered.'

According to legend (and recorded in the *Anglo-Saxon Chronicle*), the brothers Hengist and Horsa landed in Kent shortly after 449, leading a Saxon invasion, and overthrew Vortigern in 455. They set up their own kingdom in Kent and before long the Saxons were in control of much of south-eastern Britain. Archaeological evidence reveals that there was a growth in the number of Saxon settlements in the south of England at this time.

The Saxons had no written language during the fifth and sixth centuries. The principal written source is the writings of St Gildas, a monk. Sometimes known as 'Gildas the Learned', he was born in Strathclyde but spent most of his life in Wales. He wrote *The Overthrow and Conquest of Britain*. Slightly later sources are *Chronica Maiora* (725) and *Ecclesiastical History of the English People*, finished in 731, by Bede (the 'Venerable Bede', c.673–735). There is also a compilation known as *Historia Britonum* (*History of Britain*), attributed to the Welsh writer Nennius (alive around 769). The early parts of the *Anglo-Saxon Chronicle*, written in the late ninth century, are based on the writings of Bede.

Early inhabitants of Britain from about the fifth century included Angles (from Schleswig, now part of Germany) and Jutes (from Jutland, now part of Denmark). Bede named the 'Saxons' as Frisians, Rugini, Danes, Huns, Old Saxons (from Saxony) and Boructari (probably Franks), but the term 'Anglo-Saxons' came to be used for all inhabitants of Britain by the end of the ninth century.

The seven kingdoms

By the end of the sixth century, the different groups of Anglo-Saxons had begun to form kingdoms, of which seven emerged as fairly stable territories (see Generic sheet 1 on page 54). The names and the territories of three of the kingdoms have survived as modern counties:

- Essex (the kingdom of the East Saxons)
- Sussex (the kingdom of the South Saxons)

- Kent (the kingdom of the Cantiaci – the tribe that inhabited the region before the Roman and then the Saxon invasions).

The other kingdoms were:

- East Anglia (the kingdom of the East Angles), which covered the area of the modern counties of Norfolk and Suffolk
- Northumbria (the land north of the Humber), which stretched north to the Firth of Forth and west to the Irish Sea
- Mercia, which originated in the Trent valley and took over other kingdoms until it covered the area now known as the Midlands
- Wessex (the kingdom of the West Saxons), which originated in the area now covered by Hampshire and Wiltshire. Like Mercia, it took over the lands of its neighbours.

There were four main cultural groups in Britain by the seventh century:

- Celtic-speaking and -writing people in the west, southwest and Wales
- the Dal Riata Gaels in Ireland, the Hebrides and western Scotland
- the Picts north of the abandoned Hadrian's Wall
- the Anglo-Saxons in the east, from Kent to Northumbria.

Settlements grew up around the Roman towns but they did not continue the traditions, culture or way of life of the Romans.

Towards the end of the eighth century, King Offa of Mercia built his famous dyke, which marked the border between the lands of the Anglo-Saxons and the Welsh.

The Anglo-Saxons

LESSON PLAN

History objectives (Unit 6B)
- To locate the Anglo-Saxon period on a timeline.
- To recognise characteristics that place Anglo-Saxons as having lived a long time ago in the past.
- That Anglo-Saxons invaded Britain and that the period of invasion was followed by a period of settlement.
- To use the terms 'invade' and 'settle'.
- About the way of life of the Anglo-Saxons.
- To locate the Anglo-Saxon homelands on a map.

Resources

- A map of Britain on which places with Anglo-Saxon names have been fixed
- A map of Europe
- Pictures and replicas of Anglo-Saxon artefacts connected with invasion and settlement, including an axe-head, brooch, cooking pot, spindle and weaving loom weight
- Dictionaries
- A timeline on which are marked people or events with which the children are familiar
- Generic sheets 1 and 2 (pages 54 and 55)
- Activity sheets 1–3 (pages 56–58)

Starting points: *whole class*

Discuss the meanings of the words 'invade' and 'settle'. Encourage the children to look them up in a dictionary, and ask them to describe the types of behaviour of people who are invading, and those who are settling, a country. They could list verbs associated with invading, such as 'attack', 'fight', 'kill', 'seize', 'snatch' and 'take', and verbs associated with settling, such as 'build', 'create', 'entertain', 'make' and 'socialise'.

Tell the children that the Saxons came to Britain (mainly to England) from other parts of Europe, such as the lands now known as Germany, Denmark, the Low Countries and Austria, and that they arrived mainly along the North Sea coast. With help, the children could fix the names of places where the Anglo-Saxons settled on a map of England – for example, names ending in:

- burgh or brough, from *burh* meaning stronghold
- over, meaning ridge
- ham, meaning homestead
- bourne/burn, meaning stream
- den, meaning pig pasture
- ford, meaning shallow river-crossing
- ing, meaning people
- ley, meaning clearing in a forest
- ton, meaning farm or small village.

Show the children pictures of Anglo-Saxon artefacts that have been excavated and ask them to sort them into sets to indicate which items are connected with invasion and which are connected with settlement.

Help the children to place the Anglo-Saxons on a timeline. Begin by asking them if the Anglo-Saxons lived before or after other people about whom they know (for example, Florence Nightingale, Guy Fawkes, George Stephenson, and the Victorians). Point out that the Anglo-Saxons lived a very long time before any of these people and help them to count back the years (perhaps in tens).

Tell the children that they are going to read about a village called Stow. Tell them the meaning of 'Stow' ('place' or, sometimes, 'a place of assembly'). Ask the children if they know the names of any other places which include 'stow'. With the children, look at the picture of the village of Stow on Generic sheet 2. Ask:

- What kinds of houses and other buildings can you see?
- What are the buildings made of?
- Is it a modern village or an old one?
- How can you tell?
- What does it have that we do not see in modern villages?
- What do modern villages have that this one does not?

Tell the children that Stow is a reconstruction of an old village, rebuilt according to how archaeologists thought it would have looked. Read with the children Generic sheet 2. Ask them what they think made the Saxons settle in that place. Discuss what is needed for a settlement – a water supply, such as a stream or river, pasture-land for animals, and woodland for fuel and building materials.

Discuss why large groups of people moved away from places. Link this with the reasons why large groups of people move nowadays – for example, there is not enough work for them all where they live, there is a threatened danger (from nature or people), or new settlements have sprung up which attract them. Say that no one knows why the inhabitants of Stow moved away, but it is known that some other nearby villages grew in size at that time.

Tell the children that they are going to find out about Anglo-Saxon life from artefacts that have been found, together with other sources which will help them to work out what the artefacts are and how they were used.

Group activities

Activity sheet 1
This sheet is for children who are learning how to use artefacts to find out about life in the past. They match pictures of artefacts to others like them in a picture which shows them in use, and talk about how the artefacts were used. They label the artefacts and say what they think they were made from.

Activity sheet 2
This sheet is for children who can work out from artefacts (and pictures of them) how people did things and what they wore in the past. They have to identify some artefacts and explain what they were used for.

Activity sheet 3
This sheet is for children who can identify and describe the materials and the important features of artefacts from the past and relate them to other, similar artefacts with which they are familiar. They can formulate questions to help them to find out more and can use other sources to help them to identify the artefacts and to check how they were used. They have to note their observations about a number of artefacts, compose questions about them, and find the answers in a variety of other sources.

Plenary session

Ask the children what they have learned about the Anglo-Saxons and draw out that they:

- were peoples from different tribes around the parts of Europe which are now Germany, Denmark, the Low Countries and Austria
- invaded Britain more than 1,000 years ago
- built villages and settled here.

Ask the children in what ways Anglo-Saxon life was different from life today. Draw out that people then needed the same things as we do today (food and water, shelter and clothes) and talk about the ways in which they obtained those things.

Ideas for support

For children who cannot read the words for the artefacts on Activity sheet 1, ask them first to describe what they can see in each picture, draw out one main feature and what it is made of, and then talk about how it was used. Provide labelled pictures of the same artefacts and help the children to read the words and then match them to those on the activity sheet.

Provide books, pictures and electronic texts from which the children who undertake Activity sheet 3 can find out about the artefacts. To help them to use these resources, you could 'think aloud' about the process of skimming the captions of pictures.

Ideas for extension

Help the children to find out about the ways in which people lived and worked in a village such as Stow – for example, from illustrations of farming at the time and from artefacts connected with trades. From the illustrations the children can find out about the clothes worn by ordinary people and the tools they used as well as the tasks to be done each month. They could create their own display-sized 'Anglo-Saxon calendar' showing the tasks carried out on a farm.

Linked ICT activities

Discuss with the children what it would be like to move to a new town or city. Ask 'What would you miss from your old town?', 'What would you hope to find in your new town?' Discuss some of the things, taken for granted today that Anglo-Saxons would not have had (cinemas, parks, burger bars).

Ask the children what they would really need in a new town or village. Would a cinema be vital, or would it be more important to have a method of transport such as trains or buses?

Let the children use the *Local Studies* software to set up their own town (see Useful resources on page 127). The software allows the creation of a model village or town; items can be chosen to include in the model. Print the final plans and ask the children to discuss their choices (such as transport links with other places).

Make a display of the printed models and ask the children to vote for the town or village they would like to move to, and say why.

If *Local Studies* is not available, make a large plan on paper with the children. Use a word processor to create labels for the plan. Take local photographs with a digital camera (of, for example, the railway station, the cinema or shops), print them and add them to the plan.

The Anglo-Saxons

A map of the seven kingdoms

The Anglo-Saxons

The villagers had gone. The village had gone, too. It might never have been found if burrowing rabbits had not dug up some pieces of pottery. Basil Brown, the archaeologist, spotted them and was certain they were Anglo-Saxon. He began an excavation of a low hill, north of the River Lark in Suffolk, at Stow – 'place'.

All over the hill there were groups of post-holes; these were the spots where posts had been driven into the ground to support buildings. Archaeologists can work out the shapes and sizes of buildings from these holes. Other marks in the ground and tiny fragments of materials help them to work out what the buildings were used for and what they might have looked like.

Some of the buildings had planked floors and clay-based hearths, with a pit beneath the floor. All kinds of rubbish were found in these pits. Archaeologists love rubbish! It helps them to work out what a building was used for, how long ago, what people

did there, what they wore, what they ate and so on. They could tell that in one house the family pig had been kept tethered to one of the posts. They also worked out that people had first lived there in about AD420, just before the time when the Saxons invaded Britain.

The excavators found the things those people used in their daily lives: clay pottery and spindles, bone weaving pins, and more than 100 combs made of bone and antler. There were bronze brooches, pins, buckles and fasteners for clothing.

It was a lively village with about 35 families until the end of the sixth century. Then the family groups began to drift to other settlements. The buildings began to decay. They fell down, and the rubble mingled with the soil and was buried. There it stayed until Basil Brown began excavating.

The Anglo-Saxons

Draw lines to link the artefacts to those in the picture.
Write labels saying what they are and what they might have been made from.
Use the word bank to help you.

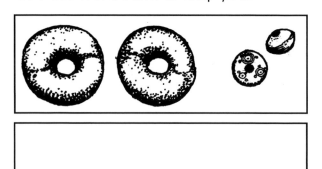

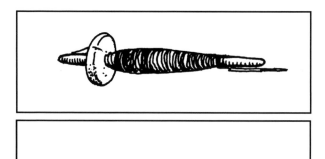

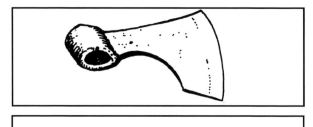

WORD BANK

axe-head   spindle   cooking pot   weaving loom weights
            iron   wood   stone

Name _____

The Anglo-Saxons

Look at the artefacts. Find them in the picture.
Write what they were used for.

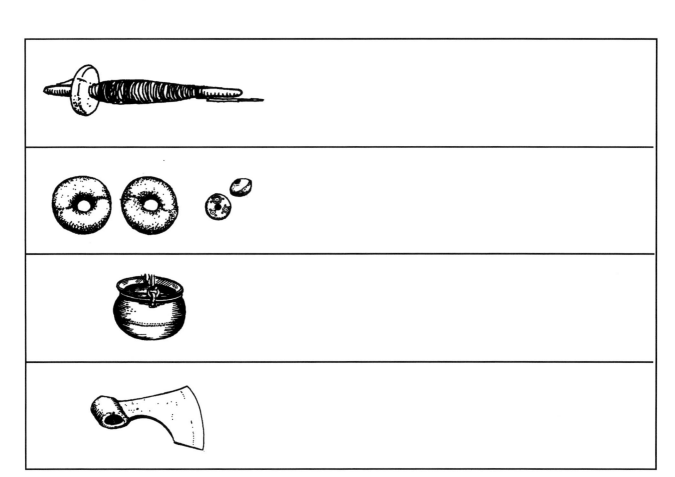

Name _____

The Anglo-Saxons

ACTIVITY SHEET

3

Look at this picture. Circle the four things listed in the table below.
Complete the table. Use books and CD-Roms to help you.

	What it was used for	My question about it	The answer I found
spindle			
loom weights			
iron pot			
axe			

PHOTOCOPIABLE

The Sutton Hoo grave

CHAPTER 6

T E A C H E R S ' N O T E S

Beginning the excavations

Sutton Hoo is on the banks of the River Deben, near Woodbridge, Suffolk. The 400-acre estate had been the home of Colonel Frank and Mrs Edith Pretty since 1926. They frequently speculated about the contents of the large grass-covered mounds on their land which, as far as they knew, had never been excavated, but they did nothing about them during the colonel's lifetime. Mrs Pretty stayed on at the estate after her husband died and, in 1938, approached the curator of Ipswich Museum to see if the mounds could be excavated professionally. Having some knowledge of, and interest in, archaeology, she had refused to allow amateur archaeologists to excavate them in case they inadvertently damaged anything.

Basil Brown, who also excavated the Anglo-Saxon village of Stow (see Chapter 5), was invited to dig the mounds. Mrs Pretty wanted him to begin with the largest one (now known as Mound 1), partly because she had had dreams in which she saw a funeral procession and then a warrior dressed for battle standing on the mound. It is said that she had employed a dowser to check the mounds; he had declared that there was gold in Mound 1.

Basil Brown was not convinced by Mrs Pretty's reasoning. He thought that Mound 1 looked as if it had been disturbed (and therefore was likely to have been plundered), and he began by excavating a smaller mound (now known as Mound 3). It turned out to have been plundered by grave-robbers. However, he found enough evidence to show that it contained the remains of an Anglo-Saxon cremation burial placed on what looked like an oak plank or the remains of a dug-out boat. There were also fragments of relief-carved bone facings, the rusted head and part of the shaft of a throwing-axe, a cast bronze lid from a jug of eastern Mediterranean origin, and part of a finely carved limestone cameo.

Brown then dug Mound 2, which had also been plundered. There he found scattered, rusted iron ship's rivets, similar to those which had been found in the 1860s at Snape (the only known ship burial in England). The outline of the wooden planks of the ship had been disturbed so much that they could no longer be clearly made out. There was also a piece of a sword blade, a gilt-bronze disc, pieces of a blue glass jar, fragments of silver-gilt foil stamped with a design (from a drinking horn) and a piece of a gilt-bronze dragon's head, thought to be from a shield.

Brown ended the 1938 dig at Sutton Hoo with Mound 4, also plundered. It contained a bronze bowl with bone remains of a female cremation with a dog and a horse.

Finding the contents of Mound 1

He did not begin excavating Mound 1 until May 1939. He soon found a ship's rivets, but this time undisturbed and still in rows. He took great care not to disturb the shape of the ship.

The burial chamber, towards the centre of the ship, had been made of oak beams with a strong gabled roof formed by two layers of planks. It collapsed when the beams rotted and the sand and soil of the mound fell in. But where was the body? Indeed, had a body ever been buried there at all? The acidic sandy soil had caused most of the organic remains to rot away, except in a few protected places. If a body had been buried there it had rotted away, but the positions of the helmet and other metal items suggest that a body could have been placed along the line of the keel, with the head at the western end.

Sutton Hoo was the main burial place during the sixth and seventh centuries of the East Anglian royal dynasty known as the Wuffing. It is still not known for sure who the burial in Mound 1 (the largest of the Sutton Hoo mounds) was for, or if he was actually buried along with the ship, since no body was found in it. The burial could have been a symbolic one – for example, if the person had been lost at sea or in battle.

What is certain is that it was the burial site of a significant warrior. But it has been suggested that, since the remains of a burial chamber were found, a body was probably interred with the ship. The most likely candidate is thought to be Rædwald, an Anglo-Saxon king who ruled from about 617 until his death in about 625.

The ship would have been buried with everything the occupant needed for the afterlife. The items buried with the body would have been the personal possessions and weapons of the person for use in the afterlife (see Chapter 7).

The land was used as a military training base in preparation for and during the Second World War. Rather than draw attention to the mounds by putting them out of bounds, they were left unmarked. Their contents were taken to the British Museum, but when war broke out they were removed, for safe keeping, to the Aldwych tunnel of the London Underground until after the war, when they could be examined properly.

At the time only 15 mounds were noticed, but Sutton Hoo has recently been re-excavated. The great ship burial is now known to have been the largest mound in a cemetery of 19 mounds and numerous other burials.

The Sutton Hoo grave

LESSON PLAN

History objectives (Unit 6B)
- To learn about what was discovered at Sutton Hoo.
- To develop an awareness of what we can and cannot learn from objects.
- To make inferences from archaeological evidence.

Resources

- A map of Britain
- Pictures of Sutton Hoo before it was excavated, the outline of the ship in Mound 1 and a reconstruction of the ship
- Different types of rivet
- Generic sheet 1 (page 64)
- Activity sheets 1–3 (pages 65–67)

Starting points: *whole class*

The children should first have completed Chapters 1 and 5.

Show the children a map of Britain and ask them to find East Anglia and the county of Suffolk. Then help them to locate Woodbridge, the River Deben and Sutton Hoo. Remind them of the areas which the Anglo-Saxons first invaded and settled in Britain and point out any Anglo-Saxon settlements about which the children know.

Tell them about Colonel Frank and Mrs Edith Pretty buying Sutton Hoo and wondering what was in the mounds. Ask the children what they think might have been in them. What would they have done if they had lived there? Discuss the problems which can be caused by people who dig carelessly or who do not know how to excavate properly. Tell them that as well as learning from the objects themselves, archaeologists can learn from the positions of things and from outlines left by things that have rotted away. Remind them about the post-holes at Stow, from which the archaeologists could tell the positions, shapes and sizes of buildings, and what they were made from.

What was in the mounds?

How do archaeologists tell, from what is left, what used to be in a place? How can they learn from things that are no longer there? Tell the children that one of the first things Basil Brown, the

archaeologist, found when he excavated the largest mound at Sutton Hoo (known as Mound 1) was an iron rivet and then another one, and then another. Show them some modern rivets and explain what they are for. Ask the children to think what the rivets in the mound might have been from.

Basil Brown carefully marked the places where he found the rivets. Ask the children if they can think why he did this. He found that they were in lines, but whatever they had held together had rotted away. Ask the children if they can work out what had been buried there. Tell them that materials like wood, leather and cloth rot away much more quickly than metals, and discuss what material the rivets might have held together and what large object could have been made of this material.

Show the children a picture of the outline of the ship that was excavated in Mound 1 at Sutton Hoo and tell them that the wooden planks had rotted away, but their outline could still be seen in the soil. The rivets that had held them together had stayed where they were since the ship was buried in about the year 625.

Read Generic sheet 1 together; this is the kind of newspaper article that appeared at the time when the mounds were excavated (in 1938–39). Ask the children what they have learned from the newspaper article which they could not learn from the picture of the ship – for example, what archaeologists already knew about the area and what they had found in some of the smaller mounds. Tell them some facts about the site: it is in a place which is known to be a burial area for a dynasty of Anglo-Saxon kings (explain the meaning of 'dynasty') known as the Wuffing; buried ships, containing bodies, armour, jewellery, money and many other artefacts, have been found in many parts of Europe, but no body was found in the Sutton Hoo ship. Discuss why no body was found there. Could there once have been a body there? What happened to it? If there was no body, why was the ship buried?

Explain that historians are still not sure why the ship was buried or whether there was a body in it, but they think it is connected with a king of the Wuffing dynasty named Rædwald. Write up the name 'Rædwald', show the children the letter 'æ', which was often used in Old English, and tell them how it was pronounced (like 'a' in 'cat'). Let them practise saying the name 'Rædwald'.

Group activities

Activity sheet 1
This sheet is for children who are beginning to understand how archaeologists find out about the past. They know that archaeologists look at things that survive from the past. They can label pictures and write simple captions. They have to draw what archaeologists discovered in the burial mound and write a caption for their picture.

Activity sheet 2
This sheet is for children who understand that archaeologists find out about the past by looking at things that survive from the past, and are beginning to appreciate the kind of care which archaeologists have to take when they dig places to look for remains. They can annotate pictures and explain their ideas. They have to draw what archaeologists discovered in the burial mound and write a caption for their picture. They are then asked to explain why these things were buried.

Activity sheet 3
This sheet is for children who understand that archaeologists find out about the past by looking at remains from the past, and know that they have to take care to make a note of the exact positions where things are found and can learn from the outlines of remains which have rotted away. The children can write notes about what they have learned and can explain their ideas. They have to complete a chart with notes about what the archaeologists discovered in the mound, then use the notes to write a short recount of the archaeologists' dig.

Plenary session

Ask the children what the archaeologists who excavated Sutton Hoo learned from the things they uncovered there and what other information helped them to know what these things were and why they might have been buried. Encourage them to share their ideas about what might once have been inside the largest mound and invite them to think of questions about the Sutton Hoo burial mounds which could be answered by using other sources. Discuss the types of sources they could use – for example, drawings, artefacts or writings from the time of the burial – and what archaeologists and historians have written about it.

Ideas for support

Talk to the children about the picture of the outline of the ship which was found at Sutton Hoo. Encourage them to follow the outlines of the planks with their fingers and to point to where the rivets which held them together might have been found. To help them to appreciate the size of it, they could chalk a life-sized copy of the ship outline on the school playground.

Reread Generic sheet 1 with the children, which will help them to draw what was inside the mound. Ask them to notice any key words and phrases that give them an idea about what might have been inside it: for example, 'cemetery', 'ship burial', 'royal burial' and 'wonderful treasures'. Explain these terms if necessary.

Ideas for extension

Help the children to use information books, electronic texts and websites to find out about ships from the seventh century. How were they different from modern ships? They could compare the materials, the sizes and shapes, and the ways in which the ships were powered.

Provide pictures from manuscripts or carvings of the time, or from artists' impressions based on archaeological evidence, of Anglo-Saxon kings and warriors. Ask the children to draw and write about what they wore and their weapons.

Linked ICT activities

Discuss with the children how exciting it must have been to uncover the Sutton Hoo treasure trove. Ask them to think about how the archaeologist must have felt discovering the buried ship. Talk about why it is important to excavate hidden treasures to find out more about the past.

Visit the *Time Team* website to find out more about the archaeologists in the programme; download sound files of them talking about their favourite finds (see Useful resources on page 127).

Imagine that the team has arrived in your school playground: they have news that there may be Anglo-Saxon remains buried there. Tell the children that they are going to write an article for a class newspaper called *Dig IT*. As reporters, they have until the end of the week to write an article to include:

- Which part of the playground was excavated? (A digital photograph could be included.)
- Which members of *Time Team* arrived to do the excavations?
- What Anglo-Saxon item did they uncover? What was it used for? (Check with your LEA guidelines on children using search engines before asking the children to search the internet for information about artefacts.)

The final article should be completed using a word processing or publishing program. Using their knowledge of fonts from Chapter 4 (see page 41), the children should use a different font for the headings.

SUFFOLK NEWS May 1939

Ship burial at Sutton Hoo

Local site gives up a royal Anglo-Saxon secret

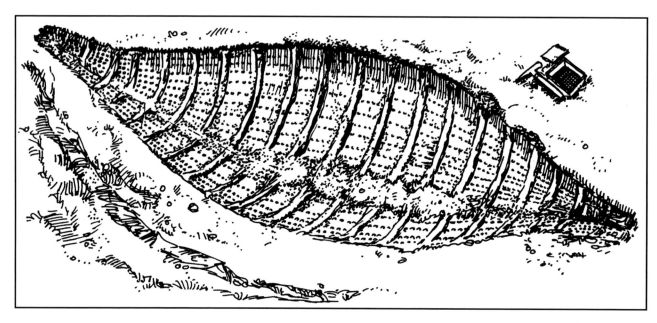

The outline of the Sutton Hoo ship, thought to be from the early seventh century

A royal cemetery has been found in the grounds of Sutton Hoo, the home of Mrs Edith Pretty, widow of Colonel Frank Pretty. Archaeologist Basil Brown and his team have found the outline of an 89-foot long ship. The ship, thought to have been for a royal burial, was at least 14 feet wide at its widest point. Its iron rivets are still in place but the wood has rotted away.

'Mrs Pretty wrote to me last year, to ask if we could send an archaeologist to excavate the mounds,' said Guy Maynard of the Ipswich Museum. 'That was when we invited Basil Brown to investigate the site.'

Mr Brown had been astonished at the size of the 15 mounds – some of them more than 70 feet long. He began digging last June.

'Last year we found the remains of a man and a horse in one mound,' he said. 'Anglo-Saxon warriors were buried with their horses. Also there were pieces of weapons, tools, pots and drinking horns.'

He had begun with the smaller mounds because they looked as if they had not been disturbed in the past. But he was wrong – they had been robbed and what was left had been scattered.

Mrs Pretty urged him to come back this year to dig the largest mound – the one Mr Brown thought had been plundered.

And that was where the ship lay. 'There are other wonderful treasures too,' said Mr Brown. These have been sent to the British Museum to be examined.

The Sutton Hoo grave

In the mound, draw what the archaeologists discovered.
Label your picture. Use the word bank to help you.

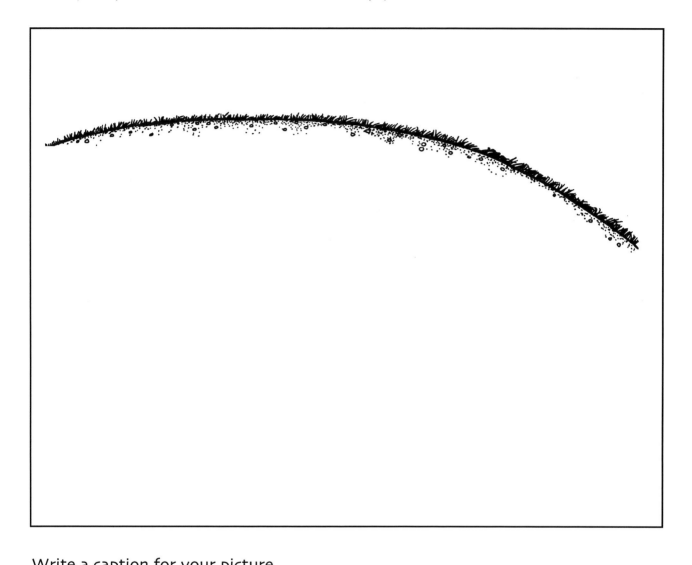

Write a caption for your picture.

_____

_____

_____

WORD BANK

earth	grass	king	planks
rivets	ship	warrior	wooden

The Sutton Hoo grave

In the mound, draw what the archaeologists discovered. Label your picture.
Write a caption for your picture. Use the word bank to help you.
Explain why these things were buried there.

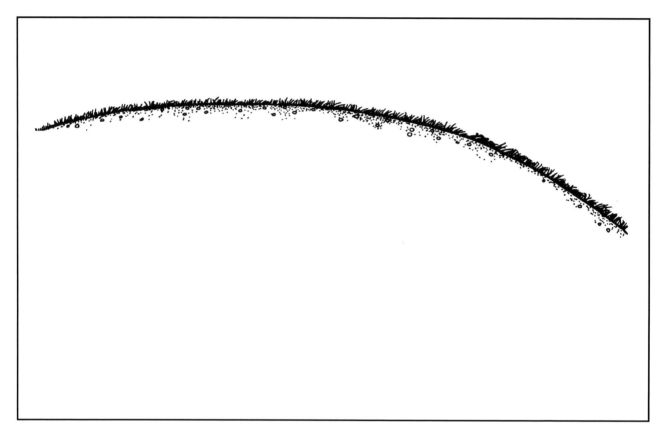

I think these things were buried because

_____
_____
_____
_____
_____
_____
_____

WORD BANK

| Anglo-Saxon | cemetery | earth | grass | iron | king |
| planks | rivets | royal | ship | warrior | wooden |

PHOTOCOPIABLE

Name _____

The Sutton Hoo grave

Write notes in the table below about what the archaeologists discovered in the mound.

What they saw *Describe what they uncovered.*	What they thought had been buried	How they could tell *Write about how they knew what the things were.*

Use your notes to write a short recount about the archaeologists' dig.

_____

_____

_____

_____

_____

_____

_____

_____

CHAPTER 7

Sutton Hoo treasures

The treasures of Mound 1

This chapter is about the artefacts that were found in the ship burial in Mound 1 (the largest mound) at Sutton Hoo during the 1939 excavations.

The outline and rivets from a ship measuring about 27 by 4.25 metres (at its widest point) were uncovered in the mound and, although no human remains were found in the collapsed burial chamber in the centre of the ship, chemical analysis showed that there could once have been a body inside. Most historians believe that Rædwald (reigned c.617–c.625), an Anglo-Saxon king of the Wuffing dynasty, was buried in, or commemorated by, the mound. He became overlord of Britain after defeating Æthelfrith, king of Northumbria, at the Battle of the River Idle, not far from Bawtry, near Doncaster (c.617). Some historians have suggested that Rædwald's son Eorpwald (d. 627/8 or 632/3) or King Ecgric (d. 635/6) might have been buried there or commemorated by the mound.

One of the written sources which mentions a ship burial is the Old English epic poem *Beowulf* (written in the eighth century). It includes a description of the burial of the sixth-century Danish king Scyld, in which similar artefacts to those found at Sutton Hoo were buried.

The Sutton Hoo artefacts from Mound 1 include:

Helmet
The iron helmet was found in pieces, much rusted, but experts at the British Museum managed to put it together (see Generic sheet 1 on page 73). It has gilt and tinned bronze plates fixed on to it, which are embossed with patterns, and below the eyebrows it has garnet inlays.

Archaeologists describe the helmet as a 'battle-mask' – it would have covered the whole of the face as well as the head and the back of the neck, and would only have been worn by a king. Close-up examination of the helmet reveals a design of boars' heads in silver wire, and the reconstruction matches well the description of a helmet described in *Beowulf*:

'Boar-images shone
above their cheek guards, covered with gold;
gleaming, tempered helmets kept guard
over the valiant men.'   (lines 303b–306a)

Sword
The rusted and broken iron blade of a sword, just over a metre long, was found in the centre of the ship, along with its gold- and gem-encrusted hilt fittings and belt mounts (see Generic sheet 1 on page 73). Gold and precious stones like garnets do not decompose in the same way as iron and, once cleaned, these stones sparkle as if they are new.

The sword has been examined and reassembled using scientific techniques. The scabbard of the sword – made of wood, leather and fabric lined with wool – became fused to the blade and was preserved by the oxides from the rusting blade. X-rays showed the blade to have been pattern-welded and of a very high quality, forged from eight bundles of seven fine iron rods, which might have been twisted before they were hammered together on an anvil. This suggests that it was meant for use in battle rather than for ceremonial purposes only.

In *Beowulf* there are descriptions of pattern-welded sword-blades: *brogden-mæl*, 'woven-blade' or 'blade with a woven pattern' (lines 1616, 1667); *wunden-mæl*, 'wounden-blade' or 'blade with a winding or coiled pattern' (line 1521b); *wæg-sweord*, 'wave-sword' or 'sword with a wavy pattern' (line 1489a).

The pommel of the sword, which is just under 4 centimetres long and about 1.75 centimetres wide at its widest point, has 53 garnets set in a delicate gold cloisonné pattern. Other small clips and fittings of similarly delicately worked material were found, which attached the sword to its hilt. They are set with tiny pieces of coloured glass and garnets set in gold. They are extremely finely worked – in some places, the details are almost microscopic. Archaeologists have been very impressed at the skill of the artisans who made them, and wonder about the tools they must have used.

Buttons

Two gold cloisonné buttons secured the top of the scabbard to the sword-belt (see Generic sheet 1 on page 73).

Large gold buckle

This gold buckle is just over 12 centimetres long and weighs about 450 grams (see Generic sheet 1 on page 73). It opens at the back (with a spring-catch which still works) to reveal a hollow section, but the purpose of this is not known. The maker cast the buckle and then worked it with a fine chisel, file and punch-hammer to create this intricate pattern. When magnified, the pattern can be seen to be made up of interlaced animals, some with the heads of eagles. The buckle was the fastener for a belt from which hung a leather purse, both of which have rotted, but enough material remains for it to be identified as leather.

Purse lid

The lid of the leather purse (see Generic sheet 2 on page 74) is made of gold and contains more than 1,500 inlays of garnet, blue glass and millefiori with gold filigree work. It is just over 15 centimetres long. On this piece the designs can be seen in the form of animals. There are hooded eagles catching smaller birds, and wolf-like animals. The eagles' eyes are made from tiny red garnets set in gold cells and inset with a minuscule bead of blue glass less than 0.25 centimetre in diameter.

Shield

Like the helmet, the remains of what was once a round shield were found in pieces. Only the metal parts survived, with traces of lime wood and leather. The reconstruction on Generic sheet 2 (see page 74) shows the decorative pieces and the boss (which also had a function in battle – for knocking the enemy to the ground). The metal decorations are made from gold, gilt-bronze, gold foil and cloisonné garnet. The boss (a domed piece of iron) is intricately decorated with gilt-bronze in the design of animals with garnet inlaid eyes. On the surface of the shield are strips of decorated gilt-bronze, an eagle of the same material with garnet inlays, and a six-winged dragon of gilt-bronze with cloisonné garnet and crystal inlays.

Gold coins

Near the purse lid 40 gold coins were found. There are 3 blank coins and 37 minted ones, each from a different mint in the kingdom of the Franks (the area now covered by France and the Rhineland). There are also two gold ingots. It seems as if the collection had been put together to represent something and to have a particular value, but it is not clear what this was or why it was done. Historians have commented that the number of coins (40) is the number of oarsmen the ship would have had, and the number of ingots matches the number of helmsmen it would have had (2). They link this with evidence from written sources that refers to the custom for the captain of a ship to have a piece of gold for every member of his crew – to placate the deities of the sea. Numismatists have dated the coins to around AD620–630, which coincides with the time of the death of Rædwald.

Silver spoons

Although ship burial was a pagan practice, some of the artefacts in this burial showed signs of Christianity – for example, two silver spoons engraved with the names 'Saul' and 'Paul' in Greek (see Generic sheet 2 on page 74). This mixture of Christian and pagan practice is consistent with what is known about the way in which Christianity was spreading through England. British Christians did not try to convert the Anglo-Saxons – Christian envoys were sent from Rome in the late sixth century to try to convert the kings. Later written sources, such as the Icelandic sagas, also describe converts to Christianity (during the tenth century) who continued to worship pagan gods in times of need.

Some historians think these spoons were gifts, probably given to mark the baptism of an adult. This is consistent with written evidence from the Anglo-Saxon scholar Bede, who wrote that Rædwald had accepted Christianity at the court of King Ethelbert, but had reverted to pagan worship on his return to East Anglia. It seems that Rædwald intended to worship both pagan and Christian gods. He had a temple with a Christian altar alongside a pagan altar.

Sutton Hoo treasures

History objectives (Unit 6B)
- To make inferences from archaeological evidence.
- About what was discovered at Sutton Hoo.
- Ask and answer questions about an archaeological site.

Resources

- Photographs or colour slides of the artefacts found at Sutton Hoo (available from the British Museum – see Useful resources on page 125)
- Extracts from *Beowulf* and children's versions of it (see Generic sheet 3, page 75)
- Activity sheets 1–3 (pages 76–78)

Starting points: *whole class*

Show the children photographs or colour slides of some of the artefacts found at Sutton Hoo. Before telling them what each picture shows, ask them what might have been the reaction of the archaeologists when they found them. What do the children think they are? Encourage them to work this out by looking for clues in the pictures and by thinking of other things the artefacts resemble.

Ask the children to describe each artefact. What can they see? What do they think it is made from? Are they surprised that people who lived some 1,500 years ago could make such delicate jewellery and ornaments, and that they are in such good condition after being buried for such a long time? This is an opportunity to develop the children's sense of awe at what people could do a very long time ago and at the splendour of the artefacts.

Help the children to use clues in the pictures or information supplied with them to find out about the sizes of the artefacts. Which of the materials are still used today? Which modern materials did the Anglo-Saxons not have? Tell the children about the materials from which the artefacts were made, which materials have survived the best and which have rotted away. Remind them about the outline which was left of the ship after the wooden planks had rotted away and tell the children about some of the ways in which archaeologists can find out about things which have rotted away. For example, they can look at the positions in which other things

were left (shoulder brooches, belt buckles and so on), test the soil for different materials, look for changes in the texture of the soil and look for tiny traces of the material. Tell the children that these methods helped archaeologists to find out that the shield was round and that it was made of lime wood covered with leather.

What can we find out from the patterns, pictures or designs on some of the artefacts? Tell the children that coin experts (introduce the term 'numismatist') could tell from the pictures and writing on the coins when and where they were minted. This helped them to work out when the ship was buried. Also mention that scientific tests are used to work out how old materials are.

After looking at the pictures of the artefacts, talk about the knowledge and other sources which archaeologists and historians drew on in order to interpret what was discovered – for example, writings about the ship burials of important people, the few historical writings from the time, other coins and other artefacts. Also discuss information that archaeologists and historians could not find from the artefacts themselves – for example, whose grave it was.

Tell the children that they are going to look at part of the Old English poem *Beowulf*, which was written in the eighth century about people who lived in the sixth century. Tell them that the poem is based on real people, although many of the events in it are made up. Explain that this is a small part of a very long poem (introduce the term 'epic'), and show them children's versions of it, which they can read at another time.

Together, read the lines from *Beowulf* on Generic sheet 3. Encourage the children to attempt to read the words they find difficult and to use dictionaries to find the meanings of any new words. Ask:

- What is the poem about?
- How does it remind you of Sutton Hoo?
- What kind of person was being buried?
- What was buried with the person?
- What clue could this give about the kind of person who was buried at, or commemorated by, the Sutton Hoo ship burial?

Tell the children that they are now going to find out about some objects buried at Sutton Hoo.

Group activities

Activity sheet 1
This sheet is for children who are beginning to learn that we can find out about people from the past from the things they left behind or that were buried with them. They are learning to ask questions that help them to find things out. They have to look at drawings of artefacts found at Sutton Hoo and decide what the artefacts tell them about the person who once owned them.

Activity sheet 2
This sheet is for children who understand that we can find information about people from the past from the things they left behind, or that were buried with them, by asking questions about those objects. They know that some questions can only be answered by finding information from other sources. They have to write notes about what they can learn from the objects shown in the pictures and write a question about each one.

Activity sheet 3
This sheet is for children who understand the kinds of information we can find about people from the past, from the things they left behind or that were buried with them. They can ask questions that help them to find this information and they know that some questions can only be answered by finding information from other sources. They understand that some questions cannot be answered with certainty and that different historians and archaeologists give different answers. They have to draw their idea of the person who owned the artefacts (tell them to include the artefacts in their picture), write notes about what they can find out from the artefacts, write some questions they cannot answer by looking at the pictures, and use other sources to find the answers.

Plenary session

Ask the children what we can learn from the artefacts buried in the ship about the person who owned them. Invite them to share their responses to the activity sheets as a basis for discussing this question. Introduce the kind of information we know from historians – that it was a king, because only kings wore this kind of helmet, and that the burial was not before the early seventh century because of the coins.

Ideas for support

Ask the children working on Activity sheet 1 what sort of person might wear armour and why. Would a woman wear armour? They might have heard of women like Boudica and Joan of Arc who led armies, but point out that in most societies in the past, men were the warriors. Ask similar questions about the other pictures. Can we tell if the person was rich or poor? How? Can we tell if he was clever? Why not?

Ask the children about how artefacts like the buckle and buttons might have been used. How do we use buckles and buttons? What kinds of materials can they be attached to? What might they fasten?

Ideas for extension

Invite the children to make up a version of a ship burial for a modern king or queen. In what could he or she be buried? (For example, a car or a plane.) What artefacts could be buried with him or her? Which things might survive the longest? Talk about what archaeologists of the future would learn from artefacts such as coins and jewellery. The children could present their ideas as a wall display or a class book.

Ask the children to make a collage of one of the Sutton Hoo artefacts, write all they can find out about it, and say what they think is special about it. These could be displayed in the form of a Sutton Hoo exhibition, which could be opened to other classes. The children could act as guides to the exhibition, explaining the artefacts to their visitors.

Linked ICT activities

With the children, look at some Anglo-Saxon treasures in more detail on the British Museum website (see Useful resources on page 125; search for 'Anglo Saxon' to access over 100 artefacts). Talk about what they were like, the types of patterns and the jewels they used.

Using a graphics package such as *Dazzle* or Microsoft *Paintbrush* (see Useful resources on pages 126 and 127), ask the children to select the drawing tool and create the outline of one of the objects, such as a buckle or a brooch. They should save the outline drawing. Ask them to reload the outline drawing and start to add detail to the object. Encourage them to use the different tools available within the program to experiment with different textures and techniques, such as the spray tool to give a speckled effect.

They should cut and paste their completed object into a word processing program, then write a short description of the object, and why they chose it. They should include: what it was used for; who it might have belonged to; where it was found. The finished pictures and descriptions could be used to add to their *Dig IT* newspaper article from Chapter 6 (see page 63).

Sutton Hoo treasures

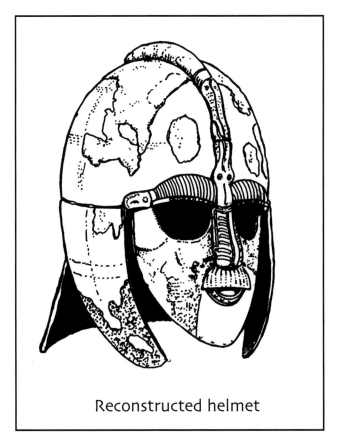

Reconstructed helmet

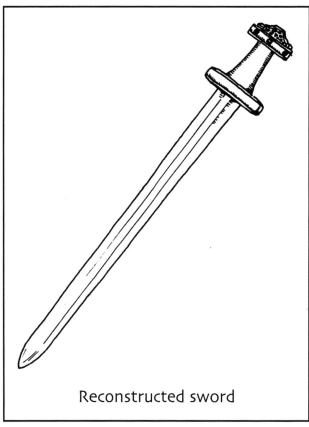

Reconstructed sword

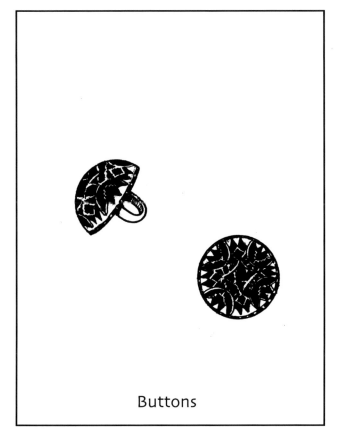

Buttons

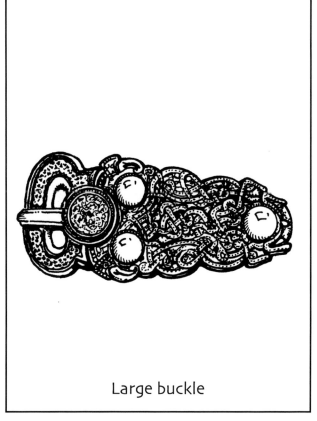

Large buckle

Sutton Hoo treasures

Lid of purse

Magnified detail from lid of purse

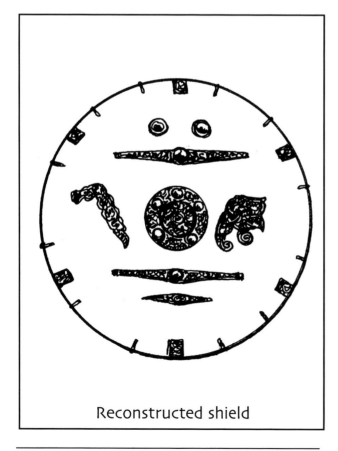

Reconstructed shield

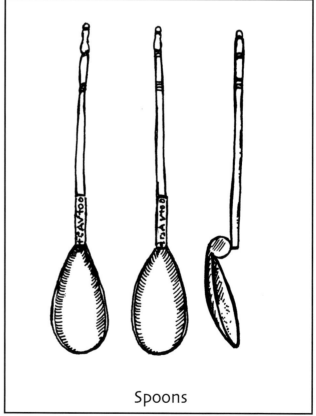

Spoons

Sutton Hoo treasures

This part of the poem *Beowulf* is about the burial of the Danish king Scyld (the father of Beowulf) in his ship. This is thought to have taken place in the sixth century.

Deep in the ship they laid him down,

Their beloved lord, the giver of rings,

By the mast in majesty. Great were the treasures there,

Far-gathered the trappings taken and set:

I never heard of a ship more fittingly furnished

With weapons of war and battle-armour,

With mail-coat and sword; there lay on his breast

Countless treasures to travel at his side,

Voyaging to the distant domains of the sea.

(lines 34–42)

Name _____

Sutton Hoo treasures

What can you learn from the artefacts?
Tick all the answers that could be right.

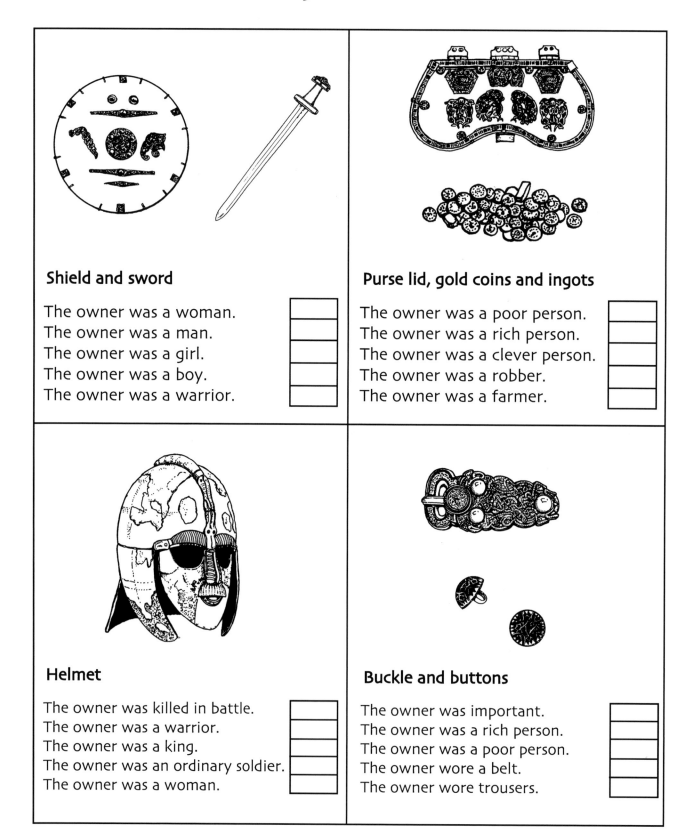

Shield and sword

The owner was a woman.	
The owner was a man.	
The owner was a girl.	
The owner was a boy.	
The owner was a warrior.	

Purse lid, gold coins and ingots

The owner was a poor person.	
The owner was a rich person.	
The owner was a clever person.	
The owner was a robber.	
The owner was a farmer.	

Helmet

The owner was killed in battle.	
The owner was a warrior.	
The owner was a king.	
The owner was an ordinary soldier.	
The owner was a woman.	

Buckle and buttons

The owner was important.	
The owner was a rich person.	
The owner was a poor person.	
The owner wore a belt.	
The owner wore trousers.	

Sutton Hoo treasures

What can you learn from the artefacts? Make notes in the table below. Write questions about the artefacts that you cannot answer by looking at them.

Artefacts	What I can learn	My question
Sword and shield		
Purse lid, gold coins and ingots		
Helmet		
Buckle and buttons		

Sutton Hoo treasures

Draw a picture of the artefacts found at Sutton Hoo and the person you think owned these artefacts.

Write down things you can find out by looking at the artefacts, as well as questions you would like to find the answers to, the answers and your sources.

A drawing of the person, with artefacts	What I can find out from the artefacts

Question	Answer	Source

The Vikings arrive

CHAPTER 8

TEACHERS' NOTES

Who were the Vikings?

The term 'Viking' is generally used to refer to the peoples of Denmark, Norway and Sweden who mounted raids on the coasts of Britain. They also went on trading expeditions to other European countries and to places as far afield as the depths of Russia. They set up settlements and trading centres and founded new and lasting colonies in the Faeroes, Greenland and Iceland; they also tried to settle in North America. To the people of those Scandinavian countries, however, the term 'viking' was used only for a young man who went off on raiding expeditions to prove his strength and courage. A more accurate term for the people themselves is 'Norse'.

The Norsemen who attacked south-eastern England were mainly Danes. Those who attacked northern and western Britain, Ireland and the Isle of Man were mainly Norwegians, while the Swedes went east into the Baltic and Russia. Their lands were overpopulated by the standards of the time and they followed the system of primogeniture, in which the eldest son inherited the family's land. These factors might have encouraged the younger sons to seek wealth, land (and even fame) elsewhere, often as 'vikings'.

These were not invasions by an organised group, as the Roman invasions had been in the first century. Groups of ships sailed together for security and greater strength but not as a national force. The *Anglo-Saxon Chronicle* records an occasion in 851 (see page 80) when 'three and a half hundred' ships sailed up the Thames

The attack on Lindisfarne

The beginning of the Viking Age is regarded as 793, with the attack on the monastery at Lindisfarne (Holy Island), but it was not the first Norse foray to England. The *Anglo-Saxon Chronicle* records:

> '787 This year King Bertric took Edburga the daughter of Offa to wife. And in his days came first three ships of the Northmen from the land of robbers. The reeve then rode thereto, and would drive them to the king's town; for he knew not what they were; and there was he slain. These were the first ships of the Danish men that sought the land of the English nation.'

When the Norsemen first came to England the country was split into different kingdoms – Northumbria in the north, Mercia in what is now the Midlands, East Anglia to the east, Kent to the south-east and Wessex to the south-west. By that time the people were Anglo-Saxons (a mixture of people of indigenous British origin with some Celts, probably some people of Roman descent or descended from people from parts of the Roman empire, as well as the Angles, Saxons and Jutes who had arrived fairly recently). Many of them worshipped pagan gods but Christianity had begun to spread after the arrival of St Augustine (late sixth century), and monasteries had been set up in places like Jarrow and Wearmouth in Northumbria.

The *Anglo-Saxon Chronicle* records the raid on the monastery at Lindisfarne as follows:

> '793 In this year terrible portents appeared over Northumbria which sorely affrighted the inhabitants: there were exceptional flashes of lightning, and fiery dragons were seen flying through the air. A great famine followed hard upon these signs; and a little later in that same year, on the 8th of June, the harrying of the heathen miserably destroyed God's church on Lindisfarne by rapine and slaughter.'

This raid was followed by several others, including more attacks on monasteries and abbeys – Wearmouth and Jarrow (Bede's old monastery), in 794, Iona in 795 and again in 802 and 806, Rathlin Island off Ireland in 795. By 799 the first raiders were also reported at various islands off the Aquitaine coast of France. But the attack on Lindisfarne was considered to be an attack on civilisation itself. An early church and monastery had been founded there in the 630s by a missionary monk, St Aidan, from another Holy Island, Iona, where St Columba had set up a church.

The arrival of the Norsemen

During the following 50 years or so the battles and bloodshed recorded in the *Anglo-Saxon Chronicle* were more frequently between different groups of Saxons rather than between Saxons and Norse raiders. However, Norsemen continued to arrive and their attacks increased in frequency between the 840s and 870s.

People assumed that the arrival of Norse ships was a raid, whether or not they came mainly to trade. But where monasteries were concerned, the intention was usually raiding, since monasteries were easy targets and contained wealth worth taking. Remember that attacks on monasteries were not the main focus of Norse raids on Britain, but they made 'headline news' because attacks on Christian holy places were considered an affront and because the written records were made by monks.

The *Anglo-Saxon Chronicle* records the following arrivals of ships of 'the heathen host' in England between 793 and 860:

Year	Place
793	Lindisfarne monastery
794	Jarrow monastery
835	Cornwall
837	Southampton and Portland, Dorset
838	Romney Marsh, Lindsey and East Anglia
840	Canterbury, Kent and Portland, Dorset
842	London and Rochester, Kent
845	The mouth of the River Parret, Somerset
851	'Wicga's stronghold' (possibly Wigborough in south Somerset), Canterbury and London
852	Thanet, Kent
855	Sheppey
860	Winchester

The first recorded settlement of Norsemen in England was in 855. After 866, fleets of Norse ships continued to arrive but the *Anglo-Saxon Chronicle* also records groups of 'the heathen men' who made peace with the Saxons, traded with them and set up their own settlements. The armies also began to move inland and northwards (as far as the River Tyne and then into the kingdom of the Picts and Strathclyde Britons) from the places where they had stayed temporarily in the south of England:

'867 Here the raiding-army went from East Anglia over the mouth of the Humber to York city in Northumbria; and there was great discord of the nation among themselves; and they had thrown down their king Osberht and accepted Ælla, an unnatural [*not belonging to the royal family*] king; and it was late in the year when they turned to making war against the raiding-army, nevertheless they gathered a great army and sought out the raiding-army at York city and broke into the city and some of them got inside; and an immense slaughter was made of the Northumbrians there, some inside, some outside, and both the kings were killed and the survivors made peace with the raiding-army.

868 Here the same raiding-army went into Mercia to Nottingham and took winter-quarters there. And Burhred, king of Mercia, and his councillors asked Æthelred, king of Wessex, and his brother Alfred to help them fight against the raiding-army; and then they travelled with the West Saxon army into Mercia as far as Nottingham, and met the raiding-army there in the fortification, and no heavy fight occurred there, and the Mercians made peace with the raiding-army.'

By 876 a Norse army had settled in Northumbria, which Halfdan (Danish king of Northumbria) had conquered in 875 and had 'divided up', and 'were ploughing and providing for themselves'.

Danegeld

Danegeld was a tax levied to provide funds for buying off Norse invaders. (The Anglo-Saxons referred to all Norse people as 'Danes', whether or not they came from Denmark.)

The Icelandic sagas

The Icelandic sagas were written mainly in the thirteenth and fourteenth centuries and were based on people and events from the early settlement of Iceland in the tenth and eleventh centuries. Literacy developed in Iceland with the coming of Christianity in about 1000. The first books written there were learned works by monks. Saga-writing developed from this, for entertainment. The sagas are stories rather than historical chronicles, but many of the events and main characters were real. They tell of the adventures of heroes, raiders and explorers and include the voyages of Leif Eiríksson in search of Vinland (part of North America).

The Vikings arrive

History objectives (Unit 6C)
- To order Viking raids in Britain chronologically.
- Where and when the Vikings raided in Britain.
- To recognise that the accounts of Norse raids from the *Anglo-Saxon Chronicle* are presented from the point of view of the Anglo-Saxons.

Resources

- Maps of Britain, Europe and the kingdoms of Britain at the beginning of the Viking Age
- Sticky notes
- A modern translation of the *Anglo-Saxon Chronicle*
- Translations and children's versions of Icelandic sagas
- A timeline that includes periods about which the children have learned
- Generic sheet 1 (page 84)
- Activity sheets 1–3 (pages 85–87)

Starting points: *whole class*

The children should first have completed Chapter 1.

Ask the children if they have heard of the 'Vikings' and, if so, what they know about them. Tell them that these 'Vikings' lived a long time ago, and help them to locate the year 793 on the timeline. Tell them that the first 'Viking' raid on Britain was recorded as having been in 793. On a map, show the children where Lindisfarne is and tell them that they are going to learn about some places the 'Vikings' attacked in Britain. Tell them that the term 'Vikings' is often used for Norsemen who sailed to Britain from northern European countries – Denmark, Sweden and Norway. Ask them to find these countries on a map of Europe.

Explain that these Norsemen began to look for other lands where they could raid, trade and settle. Point out that at that time Britain was split up into different kingdoms, which were all rivals. Show them a map of the kingdoms of Britain (see Chapter 5, page 54). Tell the children that Christians had been arriving in Britain since about the fourth century and by Anglo-Saxon times they had built churches and set up monasteries. They had converted some of the Anglo-Saxon kings to

Christianity. Tell the children that one of the monasteries was at Lindisfarne (Holy Island) off the coast of Northumbria, and was set up by St Aidan. It was a community of Christian monks. Ask:

- Why might the Norsemen have chosen to come to Britain?
- What might have attracted them?
- What might have made Britain weak?
- What made monasteries easy places to attack?
- Why were monasteries worth attacking?

Tell the children that at first the Norsemen came to raid or trade along coasts and rivers during the spring, summer and autumn months, and then they would go away, but eventually they began to stay over the winter. What do the children think happened once the Norsemen began to stay over the winter? What would they need? How might they get what they needed? (Food, clothing, everyday supplies, horses and so on.)

Discuss the ways in which the Norsemen made peace with people in some places, traded with them, bought things from them, were paid 'protection money' called 'Danegeld' to leave them in peace, and sometimes raided easy targets like monasteries. Point out that the raids on monasteries were the 'headline news' of the time, mainly because the accounts were written by monks.

Tell the children that they are going to read a text which has been adapted from another source about Norse raids. Explain that the story on which it is based is a saga and tell them what this means: 'sagas' are tales of people from the Viking Age which were told for entertainment. They had started off as tales about real people, events and places, but over the years legends were added to them and the stories were changed. They were written several centuries later. Show them some translations of the Icelandic sagas as well as children's versions of them.

Ask the children if they know where York is, and help them to find it on a map. Tell them that its Anglo-Saxon name was Eorwic. With the children, read Generic sheet 1. Compare it with the *Anglo-Saxon Chronicle's* account of the Norse conquest of York (page 80). Discuss the qualities of the leaders involved in the battle. Then ask the children to re-read the story and to find the meanings of any words or names they do not know.

Tell the children they are now going to make a timeline about some Norse raids.

Group activities

Activity sheet 1

This sheet is for children who need help in placing dates in chronological order. They have to read about some Norse raids on Britain, cut the information boxes out and put them in order on a timeline.

Activity sheet 2

This sheet is for children who are beginning to understand chronological order but need help in arranging dates on a timeline. They can find the main points in a simple text and write a short summary in the form of a headline. They have to read passages about Norsemen in Britain, write their own headlines about them and position the headlines on the timeline.

Activity sheet 3

This sheet is for children who understand chronological order and can construct a timeline with a marked scale. They can find the main points in a more challenging text and write a short summary in the form of a headline. They have to read passages from the *Anglo-Saxon Chronicle*, write their own headlines for them and make a timeline on which to glue them.

Plenary session

Ask the children what they have learned about the time when the Norsemen began to arrive in Britain and what was happening here. Some of them could present and talk about their completed timelines. Help them to locate each raid on a map of Britain and to label them using sticky notes. What do they notice about the areas that were attacked? (At first it was the north-east and then the focus was on the south and east and along the English Channel.) Tell them that the Norsemen who first came to the

north-east were mainly from Norway and that those who came later (mainly from Denmark) had already been attacking France.

What do they think the Norsemen were like? How has the *Anglo-Saxon Chronicle* affected the way in which the Norsemen have been thought of by many people? Point out that because the main sources we have of written history came from monasteries, the attacks on monasteries were 'headline news' and that these incidents give the impression that the Norsemen were anti-Christian looters who attacked only easy targets. Ask the children who completed Activity sheet 3 to share some of their headlines with the class.

Ideas for support

Ask the children to sort the dates on the reported events by the first digit only (hundreds). They will have two sets of dates. Separate the two sets and ask them to sort each set by the second digit (tens) and then by the third digit (units). Give them small pieces of scrap paper on which to copy each date. Ask them to work with a partner to put the dates in order and then to match them to those written on the timeline. They should check one another's arrangements before gluing them onto the timeline.

Ideas for extension

With the children, read passages from the Icelandic sagas and encourage them to write their own sagas about the events they have learned about from other sources, such as the *Anglo-Saxon Chronicle*.

Encourage the children to use information books and electronic texts to find out about the monasteries of the time – the monks who set them up (many of whom became saints), the kings and nobles who gave them money and land, and their collections of art, gold and silver. Also find out about the ways in which they served the community: they set up schools, produced books, helped poor people and looked after the sick. As well as being great centres of wealth they were the first centres of organised scholarship in Britain.

The more able children could write headlines from the point of view of the Vikings.

Linked ICT activities

Start by displaying headings on a blank wall or pinboard, such as:

- Who were the Vikings?
- How did they live?
- What did they look like?

Then ask the children to research using the internet and the list of appropriate sites given in Useful resources on pages 126 and 127.

Each day, add a new question to the display. Encourage the children to add their findings to the display, including other useful websites and resources they find (with adult supervision).

If your school has a website, the children's information could be collated to create a content area for Vikings/Norse people. Share the content with other schools by letting the teachers know that it is on your site, and by encouraging the children to email their friends in other schools. Email links with schools in other countries would be useful, possibly to provide further information about the Norse people.

The Vikings arrive

There was a man named Ivar the Boneless. He had raided far and wide in Ireland. He had two brothers: Halfdan of the Wide Embrace, and Ubbi. They were the sons of Ragnar Hairy Breeks. In the year 865 they led a Danish army on a raid to England.

They landed their boats in East Anglia. They made peace with the people there, who sold them horses, and they stayed there for the winter. Meanwhile old Ragnar Hairy Breeks led a raid on Northumbria. Ælla, the king, captured him. 'Who is this man?' he asked. But Ragnar would not give his name. Ælla threw him into a pit of poisonous snakes to make him talk. The snakes bit him and, as he died, he sang the Death-Song of Ragnar: 'Down we hewed them with our swords!'

The sons of Ragnar rode northwards with their warriors. On All Saints' Day they came to Eorwic (York), the capital of Northumbria. The city was full of worshippers, revellers and traders enjoying the festival. The people of Northumbria were busy fighting one another. Some supported Ælla as king and some supported Osberht, who had been thrown out. So hardly a soul noticed the band of Norsemen slipping into the city. 'We shall take a few of these fine old Roman buildings,' said Ivar. So they patched up the ruined buildings and moved in.

Then Ælla and Osberht became friends. The Northumbrians joined forces against the Norsemen.

But the Vikings slaughtered them. Then the sons of Ragnar heard what had happened to him. 'We must avenge our father,' they said.

So they carved a 'blood-eagle' on Ælla's back to dedicate him to their god Odin. This is what they did: Ivar the Boneless hacked his ribs from his spine and pulled out his lungs; then he spread the lungs across his ribs like wings.

After that the Norsemen tidied up the mess and settled down. Eorwic became Jórvík.

Name _____

The Vikings arrive

Read about the Viking raids on England in the boxes below. Cut them out. Put them in order and glue them onto the timeline.

867 Viking army takes York.

793 Viking raid on Lindisfarne monastery.

852 Battle against Vikings on Thanet.

865 People of Kent pay Vikings to be peaceful, but Vikings go raiding that night.

794 Vikings raid monastery at Jarrow in Northumbria.

837 Saxon army defeats Vikings at Southampton.

855 Viking army in Sheppey over winter.

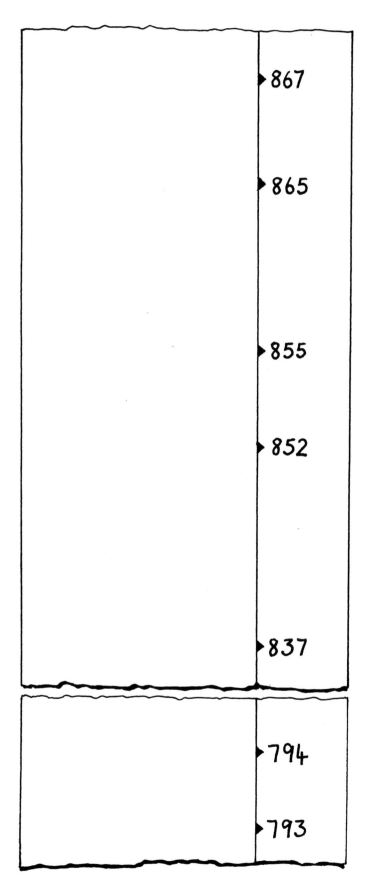

867 865 855 852 837 794 793

865

855

852

837

794

793

The Vikings arrive

Read about the Viking raids on Britain in the boxes below and put the events in chronological order. On the timeline, write a headline for each event.

867 The raiding army went from East Anglia to York and broke into the city. They slaughtered many Northumbrians there and killed King Osberht and King Ælla.

837 Ealdorman Wulfheard led a victorious army against 33 ship-loads of Vikings at Southampton. Many on both sides were killed.

793 Viking ships landed in Northumbria and the Vikings looted the monastery at Lindisfarne and killed many of the people there.

855 For the first time a Viking army stayed in England over the winter – in Sheppey.

865 A Viking army stayed on Thanet and the people there said they would pay them if they would not fight them. But the Vikings crept away at night and raided across all eastern Kent.

852 Ealhere of Kent and Huda of Surrey led their forces against a Viking army on Thanet. Many on both sides were killed.

794 A Viking force raided the monastery at Jarrow in Northumbria. One of their commanders was killed and some of their ships were broken up by storms.

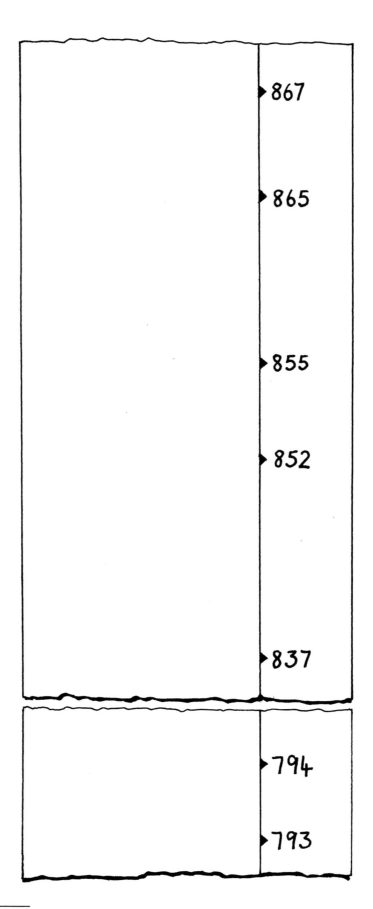

PHOTOCOPIABLE

The Vikings arrive

Read these passages from the *Anglo-Saxon Chronicle* and discuss what they mean. Cut out the passages and put them in chronological order. Write a headline for each event. Make a timeline and stick the recounts and their headlines onto it.

852 Ealhere with the inhabitants of Kent, and Huda with the Surrey men, fought on Thanet against a heathen raiding-army; and many were killed and drowned there on either side, and the ealdormen both died.

855 The heathen men for the first time settled in Sheppey over winter.

865 The heathen raiding-army stayed on Thanet, and made peace with the inhabitants of Kent; and the inhabitants of Kent promised them money in return for that peace. And under cover of the promise of money, the raiding-army stole away by night and raided across all eastern Kent.

794 The heathen raided in Northumbria and looted Ecgfrith's minster at the Don mouth [Jarrow]; and there one of their commanders was killed, and also some of their ships were broken up by bad weather, and many of them drowned there; and some came to shore alive, and then were immediately killed at the river mouth.

793 In this year terrible portents appeared over Northumbria which sorely affrighted the inhabitants: there were exceptional flashes of lightning, and fiery dragons were seen flying through the air. A great famine followed hard upon these signs; and a little later in that same year, on the 8th of June, the harrying of the heathen miserably destroyed God's church on Lindisfarne by rapine and slaughter.

867 The raiding-army went from East Anglia to York city in Northumbria; and there was great discord among themselves; and they had thrown down their king Osberht and accepted Ælla, an unnatural king; and it was late in the year when they turned to making war against the raiding-army. Nevertheless, they gathered a great army and sought out the raiding-army at York city and broke into the city; and an immense slaughter was made of the Northumbrians there, and both the kings were killed, and the survivors made peace with the raiding-army.

CHAPTER 9

Norse ships

The role of ships in Norse culture

This chapter is about the different kinds of ships the Norsemen used for war and trade. Pictures and carvings from the time and the remains which have been excavated show different types of ships which were designed for different purposes:

- ships for sailing long and short distances (including sailing up rivers)
- merchant ships
- warships.

What distinguished Norse ships from others of the time was that they were lighter, slimmer and faster.

Ships were an important part of the culture of the Norse people. In Norway and Sweden most people lived near the coast or large lakes; waterways such as fjords were sheltered and they were routes to the sea. Denmark is mainly a collection of islands, between which communication was naturally by sea. According to Peter Sawyer in *The Oxford Illustrated History of the Vikings*:

> 'These natural features also meant that the authority of many rulers in Viking Age Scandinavia, unlike that of their contemporaries in Europe, to a large extent depended on ships and control of the sea.'

A ship was also a status symbol; a fine ship conferred prestige on its owner; there are many instances in the Icelandic sagas of gifts of a ship to confer high honour on a person. Important people were buried in their ships after they died and ships were depicted on coins (see below).

Coins depicting Norse ships

Norse shipbuilding

Norse ships were built hull first and the frames were added later, unlike modern wooden ships, whose hulls are built by fixing planks on to a frame. The keel was built first and then the bow and stern posts were added. The hull was 'clinker-built' (built up from overlapping planks fastened by iron rivets) and was made watertight by pressing wool, cattle hair, cloth or plant fibres and moss into the spaces between the planks and then by tarring the outside.

As the hull was completed, internal strengthening frames were fitted. The mast was fitted in a 'mast-step'. This was a long, heavy timber designed to spread the load of the mast and sail over a large area of the keel and hull. The ship was completed by adding decking, a sail, rigging and a side rudder (always on the right – 'steerboard', hence 'starboard').

Unseasoned wood was used for building ships because it was easier to work than seasoned wood. Planks were never sawed; they were cut by splitting logs lengthways. This made the best use of the wood's natural strength and flexibility and minimised the shrinkage as the wood seasoned. The planks were finished with an axe.

Warships

The term 'longship' is used loosely to refer to warships. These were designed for transporting armies and raiding parties. Warships were primarily galleys (boats for rowing) so that they could be used without wind, although they also had a mast, which could be lowered, and a single square sail. Lowering the mast helped to render the ship less easily spotted by an enemy; it was also more convenient during a sea-battle.

Longships could move very quickly powered by sail or oars. Ships such as the Skudelev 5 from Denmark had a shallow draught (less than half a metre fully loaded) which made it easy to manoeuvre and ideal for use in shallow coastal waters and rivers, but not in rough seas.

Very large longships called *drakkars* (dragons) came into use later in the Viking Age and were mainly owned by kings. They were designed for use in the open sea, with high prows and sides, which made boarding more difficult and enabled their crews to shoot downwards onto smaller enemy ships. They had 30 benches (that is, 60 oars) or more.

Merchant ships

Knörrs were merchant ships. They were shorter and broader than warships, and had deeper and heavier hulls for carrying cargo, and permanently fixed masts. They were sailing ships, although they carried some oars for manoeuvring in and out of harbours. They were slower and more difficult to manoeuvre than longships. (See Generic sheet 1 on page 93.)

The knörr was the main Norse merchant ship. This is thought to have been the type of ship used for the voyages of settlement and exploration in the North Atlantic. The largest known knörr was found in the harbour at Hedeby in Denmark. It measured 25 metres in length, 5.7 metres in width and was 2.5 metres deep, with a cargo capacity of 38 tonnes.

Norse ships

History objective (Unit 6C)
• To use a range of sources to find out about Viking longboats.

Resources

- Information books about, and pictures of, Norse ships that have been excavated by archaeologists
- Pictures and information from books, museums and websites about reconstructions of different types of Norse ships
- A set of pictures of different Norse warships and merchant ships (from museums and websites); include photographs and drawings of the remains of ships and reconstructions as well as pictures and carvings from the Viking Age
- A prepared word bank format (lettered A to Z)
- Generic sheets 1–3 (pages 93–95)
- Activity sheets 1–3 (pages 96–98)

Starting points: *whole class*

The children should first have completed Chapters 1 and 8.

Show the children pictures of Norse ships of different types and tell them how we know about these ships. Generic sheets 1 and 2 show a merchant ship and a longship. Show them pictures and carvings of ships from the time (for example, the Gotland picture-stones), pictures of the remains of ships that archaeologists have found and pictures of reconstructions (see Useful resources, page 125).

Discuss how the ships were made to move (introduce the term 'power source'), the main source of power, how the ships were steered and whether they were mainly for carrying people or goods. Write the words 'oar', 'row' and 'sail' on a prepared word bank, which the children can use for reference. Do the children know how the sailors steered the ships? Point out the rudder. Tell them that it was on the right-hand side of the ship, and explain the origin of 'starboard' ('steerboard').

Give the children sets of pictures of Norse warships and merchant ships and introduce the terms 'warship', 'merchant ship' and 'trading ship'. Ask them to sort the ships into two sets – warships and merchant (trading) ships. Tell them that the word

'longship' is used for Norse warships and discuss why. Tell them that the word for a large merchant ship was 'knörr'. Write these words in the word bank.

Ask the children to look at details in the pictures of ships. Compare them with pictures of other ships that were heavier and less streamlined. Discuss which ships would be the easiest to manoeuvre and which would be the fastest and why.

Draw the children's attention to the ships' masts. Longships had a mast that was fixed in such a way that it could be lowered. Discuss why this was useful – a longship was used mainly in inland waters and for short distances and it was usually rowed, which meant that it did not depend on wind, but the sail could be used if needed. Point out that a knörr was a sailing ship with a fixed mast. It could be used for longer distances and open seas.

Also draw the children's attention to the differences between the hulls of the different types of ship and ask them which would stand up better to rough seas and which would be easier to sail quickly around coasts and up rivers. Ask:

- Why did the Norsemen have different kinds of ship?
- What were the names of the different kinds of ship?
- How were they used?
- How were they powered?
- What was special about their shape?

Read Generic sheet 3 with the children and encourage them to try to read any words that are new to them and to use the context to work out what they mean. Then ask them to reread the page with a partner and to suggest materials that they could use for making a model of a longship for each stage shown on the sheet. Ask them to annotate the pictures to show the materials they could use, how big they could make their models and how they could join the materials. If possible let them use a computer to look at a website showing reconstructions of Norse ships – for example, Vestrus Viking Ships at www.vestrusvikingships.org/faering.htm. They can find out from this site details such as how the planks (strakes) are joined by rivets and how the mast is attached to the ship. They could make their models during another lesson.

Tell the children they are now going to find out more about Norse ships.

Group activities

Activity sheet 1
This sheet is for children who, with help, can find information from pictures. They know that one type of Norse ship was a longship and that this type of ship was used as a warship. They have to use the new vocabulary they have learned about ships to label a picture and to complete sentences about the ship.

Activity sheet 2
This sheet is for children who can find information from pictures and compare two pictorial sources. They have to compare pictures of a longship and a merchant ship, label the pictures and fill in a chart about the similarities and differences between the two types of ship. They need copies of Generic sheets 1 and 2 for reference.

Activity sheet 3
This sheet is for children who know how to use a range of information texts and pictures to find specific information. They have to use various sources to find out about longships and merchant ships, then fill in a chart to compare the two types of ship.

Plenary session

Ask the children what they have learned about Norse ships. Ask:

- What were the main types of ship?
- How were they similar?
- How were they different?
- What made the Norsemen's ships better than other ships of the time?
- How were the ships made?
- Were you surprised at the order in which the parts of the ship were assembled?

Ideas for support

Encourage the children to add new words to the word bank that was started at the beginning of the lesson, and to use it to check the spellings of words. Ask them to point to any words in the word bank whose meanings they have forgotten, especially parts of the ships. Help them to find those parts of the ship on a picture. If necessary, make a picture dictionary of ship parts.

Ideas for extension

Ask the children to make small models of Norse ships, based on the notes they have made. You could help them to mark out and make a large-scale model of a Norse ship (dimensions are given on several websites about the ships and in books such as *The Oxford Illustrated History of the Vikings*, which has an entire chapter devoted to ships – see Useful resources on page 125).

Using a large-scale model as a prop, the children could enact the voyages of the Norsemen, for both raiding and trading. Encourage them to use information books to find out about the goods that were traded and the weapons that the Norsemen used during their raids.

Linked ICT activities

Discuss with the children how the Norsemen built their ships (use Generic sheet 3 on page 95). Talk about how we use lists of instructions to make things today, such as a model toy or a piece of furniture. How are these instructions written? (Bullet points, numbered lists.) Show the children some instructions, or ask them to find some around the classroom or the school. Talk about the use of pictures and diagrams, which help to explain the instructions.

Discuss whether or not the Norse shipbuilders would have followed instructions like these. If not, how would they know how to build the ships?

Ask the children to use a word processing program to produce a set of instructions explaining how to build a Norse ship. They should use a numbered list or a bulleted list. Provide copies of Generic sheet 3 *without the text*, talking with them about each picture before they start to write.

Ask the children how they think modern technology is used to help create plans for building ships, and to test the plans. Talk about how computers are used to generate ship designs, and then to create models for testing the designs (such as finding out whether the ship will roll over in bad storms or high tides).

Ask the children to research other facts and information about Norse ships. They can use CD-Roms, but check with your LEA guidelines on children using search engines (some LEAs provide them for schools) before asking the children to search the internet for information.

Norse merchant ships

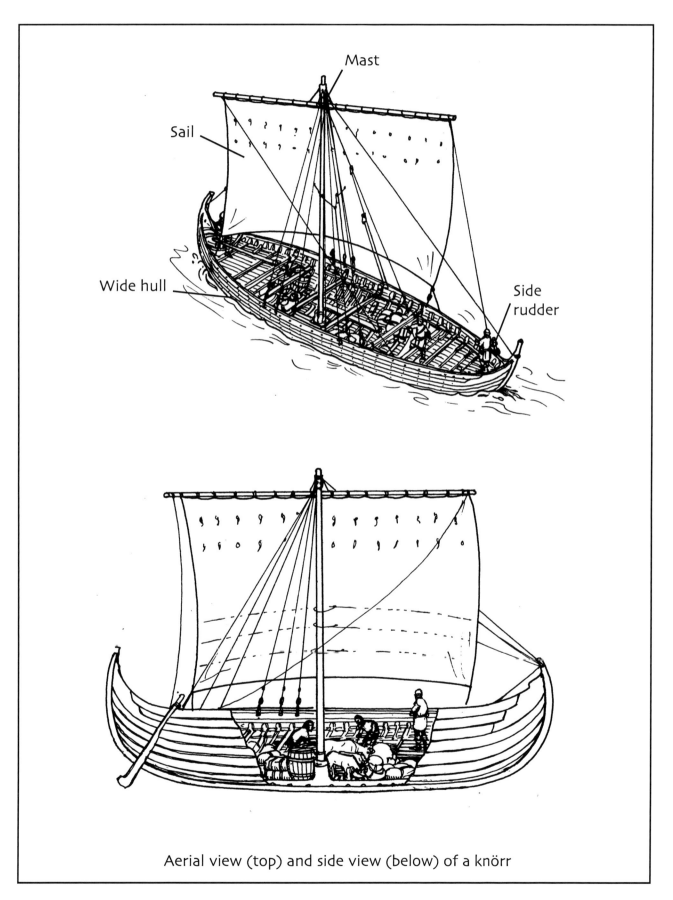

Mast

Sail

Wide hull

Side rudder

Aerial view (top) and side view (below) of a knörr

Norse longships

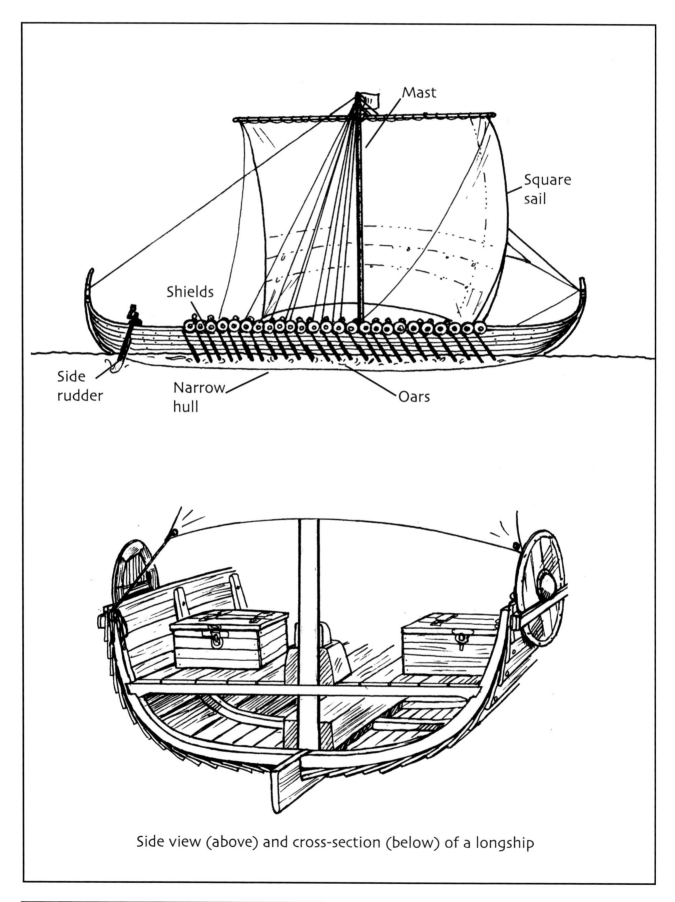

Side view (above) and cross-section (below) of a longship

Labels on the side view:
- Mast
- Square sail
- Shields
- Side rudder
- Narrow hull
- Oars

PHOTOCOPIABLE

Building a Norse ship

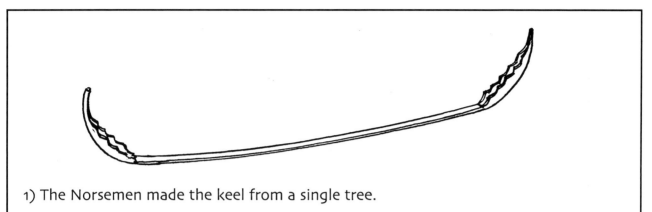

1) The Norsemen made the keel from a single tree.

2) The hull is made from planks, called strakes, beginning by joining a strake to each side of the keel. The next strakes are joined to these two until both sides are built up.

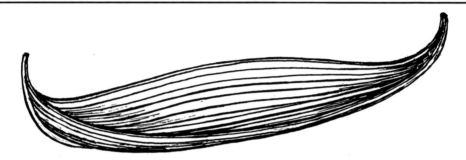

3) Ribs are made to fix the shape of the hull. The crossbeams are placed on top of the ribs to support the deck planking.

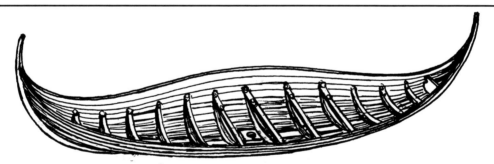

4) The mast, sail and rudder are fitted. The mast is fixed on in a way which allows it to be taken down.

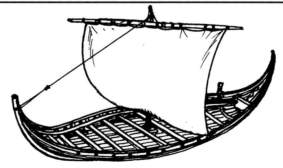

Norse ships

Label this picture of a Norse longship. Then fill in the gaps in the sentences.
Use the word bank to help you.

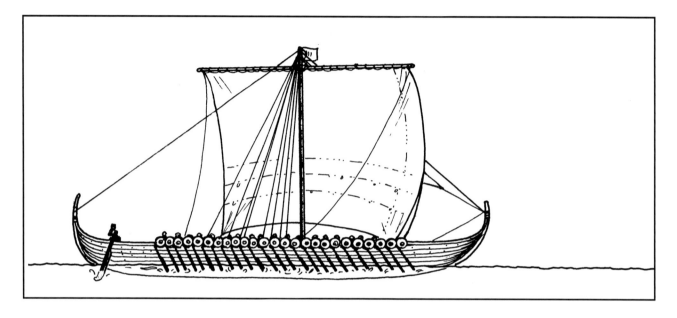

A longship is a type of w_____ship.

The longship is very st_____. It is very l_____. These
things make it a very f_____ ship.

People r____ the ship to make it move. They use o_____. If the sailors
want to use the wind for power they put up the m_____. They fix the
s_____ to the mast. They can take the mast d_____ if they do not
need it.

The ship has one sail. Its shape is s_____.

```
                          WORD BANK
    fast        mast        sail        war        down

    oars        square      light       row        streamlined
```

PHOTOCOPIABLE

Name _____

Norse ships

Label the pictures of the Norse longship and merchant ship.
Use Generic sheets 1 and 2 to help you.
Look for the similarities and differences between them and fill in the table.

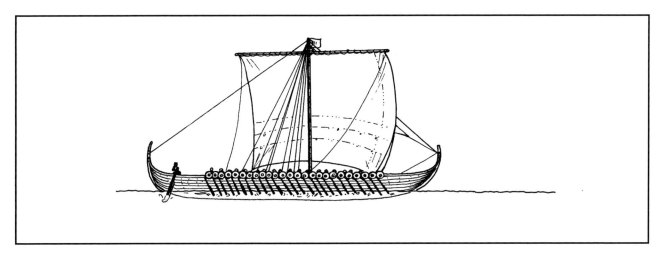

Similarities	Differences

Name _____

Norse ships

Look at the pictures and use other sources to find out about Norse longships and knörrs. Write notes in the table about the two kinds of ship.

A longship is a type of warship. A knörr is a merchant ship.	Longship	Knörr
What it was used for		
Shape of hull		
Depth of keel		
How it was powered (the main way and any other ways)		
The mast		
Important features		

Norse settlements

CHAPTER 10

TEACHERS' NOTES

Buildings

The town houses of Jórvík (York) were closely packed together with a small yard (sometimes containing a privy) surrounded by a wattle fence. Most of the buildings from the Viking Age that have been excavated in York were of timber and wattle and daub with roofs of reed or straw thatch, although a few important buildings, such as churches or royal residences, were wholly or partly stone-built. For storage, outbuildings were attached to houses and workshops. There were no chimneys, but openings high up in the gable ends allowed smoke from the hearth to escape. Floors consisted of trodden earth, which could be covered with reeds or straw. There were few openings in walls and roofs (in order to retain warmth), and so the interiors of buildings would have been quite dark. The remains of one house in York contained a mixture of brushwood and willow twigs, which was thought to be a type of cavity wall insulation used until fairly recently in Denmark (wood wool).

Some smaller, poorer dwellings had only one room with a hearth in the centre, used for heating and cooking, and sleeping platforms (made of earth, faced with wooden boards), also used as seating, against the side walls. Larger houses had several sleeping alcoves furnished with rugs, pillows and furs. These had furniture such as low stools, chairs, a feasting table, benches and lockable storage chests. A nobleman's or wealthy merchant's house may have had doors, door posts and gable end bargeboards with carved decorations, and the inside walls may have been hung with tapestries. To light their homes and workshops the people of Jórvík used simple oil lamps (carved from stone or made from clay) or tallow candles. Richer people used wax candles. Most of the light came from the fire.

Cooking

Over the fire there would be a metal or wooden frame from which cooking vessels could be suspended and – in the homes of richer people – an iron spit to support meat for roasting. Sometimes there would be a domed clay oven at one end of the house, or perhaps outside it. Some houses had a pit beside the fireplace on which food could be fried over the hot ashes scraped out of the hearth. Various household utensils such as knives, clay and iron pots and pans (including a wooden-handled iron frying pan) have been unearthed, as well as querns for grinding corn. Baskets, buckets and pottery jars were used for storing foodstuffs, and most homes had a kettle made of iron or clay in which a meal was cooked (the remains of stew have been found clinging to pieces from these kettles).

Spoons and ladles made of wood and bone and iron knives have been found, but the only forks were large ones used in cooking (for fishing out pieces of meat from the kettle). Large shards of pottery that have been unearthed are thought to have been used for moving hot ash and stones, or for baking flatbread.

Food

Remains found in Jórvík suggest that the people there had enough to eat even in the winter. They ate the meat of domesticated animals (beef, pork, mutton, lamb, chicken and goose) and sometimes of hunted animals and birds (notably deer, hares, moorland birds, woodland birds and waterfowl). They also had shellfish as well as river and sea fish. Other sources of protein were eggs from the poultry they kept and nuts such as hazelnuts and walnuts.

We cannot be certain exactly what the meals were like in Jórvík but there is a great deal of evidence of the raw materials. The remains of the food have been found on utensils such as pots and knives. Also the stomachs and intestines of some of the well-preserved human remains found in bogs have been examined to find out what their last meal was.

The people of Jórvík made bread from barley, buckwheat, oats, rye and wheat; they also made oatcakes called 'havercakes' or 'haverbread'. Cereal grains were 'creed' (steeped) in milk, or a mixture of milk and water, to soften them before they were cooked as porridge. They sweetened their food with honey, which was also fermented to make mead. The other popular drinks were beer and wine.

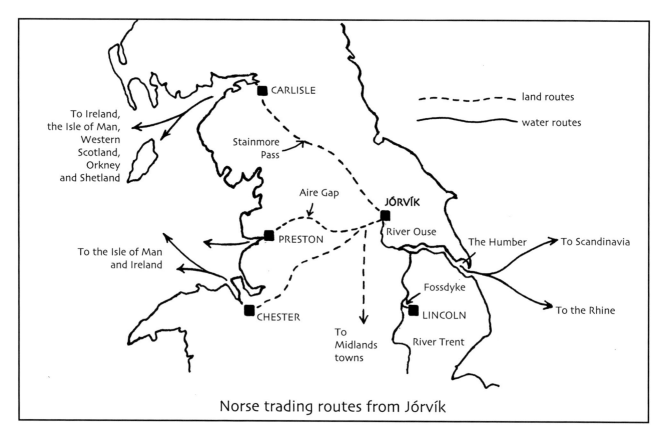

Norse trading routes from Jórvík

Some homes had vegetable gardens in which they grew angelica, beans, carrots, hops, onions, parsnips and peas. Other vegetables eaten included beetroot, cabbage and leeks, as well as fruits and berries including apples, blackberries, cherries, dewberries, elderberries, haws, plums, raspberries, rowanberries and sloes. Berries, acorns and nuts could be gathered from nearby woodlands.

Clothes

Wool was the most commonly used material for making clothes. The women spun and wove the wool at home and dyed the cloth with mineral and vegetable dyes. They also made clothes from linen, made from flax, which also had to be spun and woven. The remains of upright weaving looms, stone loom weights, and bone weaving tablets for weaving braid have been found in Jórvík (see Generic sheet 1 on page 105).

Men wore a sleeved jerkin or a three-quarter belted coat over a long woollen shirt and long cloth trousers held up by a sash or drawstring. They wore woollen socks and soft leather shoes or boots. Women wore a long woollen tunic, rather like an apron, over a long linen dress, which might be either plain or pleated. The tunic was suspended at the shoulders by a pair of brooches, sometimes

joined by a chain or string of beads (like the roughly-cut amber ones found at Jórvík). Some wore a shawl. Like the men they wore woollen socks and soft leather shoes. Both men and women wore fur or woollen hats and cloaks in cold weather. The cloaks were fastened at the shoulder with a brooch or a pin.

Jewellery found at Jórvík includes strings of amber and glass beads, engraved silver armlets, bracelets and rings and the ends of belts or straps made from engraved bone, which was sometimes dyed a greenish colour.

Crafts and trades

The materials and tools found in the remains of some buildings suggest that they were workshops in which craftspeople made artefacts and utensils from a variety of materials.

Antler and bone
Objects made from antler and bone are very common finds in Jórvík. Many were home-made: simple whistles, toys, ice skates, toggles for fasteners, spindle weights and needles. Musical instruments such as lyres and flutes, and combs fashioned from antler, required a higher level of skill; these were more likely to have been made by craftsmen.

Metals

The remains of a blacksmith's forge and tools were uncovered at Jórvík. He would have made the metal tools found in several buildings (pliers, axe-heads, keys, drills and cutters of various types) as well as the household utensils that have already been described. A coin-maker's materials, such as blank coins and dies in which coins were stamped, were also uncovered. It appears that only pennies were used: if a smaller value was required the coin was cut in half or into quarters. Numerous neatly-cut halves and quarters of coins have been found.

Clay

Evidence from Jórvík shows that there were several potters in the town. Clay pots were stacked in kilns dug into the ground and covered with a domed roof of stone, earth and turf. A furnace in an adjoining pit, fuelled by wood or charcoal, heated the kiln to fire the pots.

Leather

Some very well preserved shoes and a wooden last were found in the remains of a shoemaker's workshop at Jórvík. Leather uppers were stitched onto leather soles. Some of the shoes were in the style of pull-on boots and others were fastened with leather thongs.

Wood

Coppergate (from Old Norse *koppr*, cup, and *gata*, street) is the street of woodworkers. Wooden tableware from Jórvík survived well in underground waterlogged places. Tableware such as plates, cups and bowls was mostly made by woodworkers who had mechanically operated lathes (pole lathes) similar to those used by the Anglo-Saxons. Other wooden items which were found include buckets and tubs made from staves bound with hoops of wood or metal, spoons, ladles, knife-handles, handles for metal cooking pots, mortars, pestles, trays, lids, stoppers, butter churns and cheese presses.

Norse settlements

History objectives (Unit 6C)
• To make inferences about the Viking way of life.
• To ask and answer questions from archaeological evidence.

Resources

• A map of Britain
• Pictures of artefacts found during the excavations of York, or pictures of similar artefacts from information books and websites
• Ideally, replicas of the artefacts (see Useful resources on page 126)
• Ideally, samples of any materials with which the children might be unfamiliar: for example, amber, antler, bronze
• Pieces of unfired clay which the children can shape
• A picture of a potter's wheel
• Generic sheet 2 (page 106)
• Activity sheets 1–3 (pages 107–109)

Starting points: *whole class*

The children should first have completed Chapters 1, 8 and 9.

Tell them that they are going to look at some of the things that archaeologists found when they excavated the ground beneath Coppergate, a street in York. Help them to find York on a map. Point out that the archaeologists could tell from how deeply things were buried and from scientific tests (as well as their knowledge of other findings) which buildings and artefacts were from the time of the Norse settlement of York. Remind the children that the Norse name for York was Jórvík.

Show them pictures and, where possible, replicas of artefacts that were excavated at Coppergate in York – for example, a cooking pot, bone needles, shoes, clothing (including socks), jewellery, coins (including coins which had been cut into pieces), coin dies, and musical instruments. Ask the children to answer the following questions by looking at the artefacts and pictures:

• What materials did the Norse people use for making things? Build up a list. Ensure that the following are included, and explain any with which the children might be unfamiliar, or show them samples: amber, antler, bone, clay, glass, leather, linen, metals (bronze, gold, iron and silver), wood and wool.

• What materials do we have today that the Norse people did not have? Ask the children to name as many as possible – for example, paper, plastic, porcelain and rubber. Encourage them to check all the available sources to see if they are right. They might be surprised that glass was available, since there were no glass windows in the buildings.

• What kinds of clothes did they wear? Find out from the sources about the styles of their clothes, how they were made and by whom. Show the children pictures or replicas of bone ice skates and explain how they were fixed to the feet (using thongs threaded through holes drilled in the skate at the back and front). Tell them that people have tested some of these skates and found them to be still usable.

• Did the Norse people have clothes made from cotton, nylon and silk? Help the children to check for examples of these, or for information which shows that they could not have had them (for example, nylon had not yet been invented). Look for surprising facts – for example, they had silk. Show the children the trade routes from York to other parts of Britain and the world, and remind them about the merchant ships about which they learned in Chapter 9.

• Did they wear jewellery? What was it made of and what did it look like? Note the use of brooches to support women's tunics worn over long dresses, and beads which were sometimes worn suspended from the brooches or round the neck. Look at pictures of finger- and arm-rings and bracelets. Show the children a sample of amber and tell them where it comes from (refer to the trade routes again).

- Did the Norse people play musical instruments? What were they like? Show them pictures or replicas and tell them that a set of panpipes found at Coppergate was tested and found to be still capable of producing musical sounds.

Tell the children that they are going to learn about the work of a potter in Jórvík. Discuss their experience of making pots. What materials are used? How is the pot shaped? Show them a replica pot (or picture of one) from Jórvík and let them try shaping some clay. Discuss how easy or difficult it is to make it into the shape of a pot like the one from Jórvík. Show the children a picture of a potter's wheel and ask them to look closely at the pot from Jórvík. Are there any clues to suggest that it might have been made using a wheel? Point out the horizontal lines around it which were made by the potter's fingers as he shaped it on a wheel.

Read Generic sheet 2 with the children and encourage them to identify the main stages in the making of the pot. The children could collaborate in a shared writing activity: writing instructions for making a pot.

Tell the children they are going to find out more about a Norse pot from Jórvík.

Group activities

Activity sheet 1
This sheet is for children who can look for a list of features on an artefact and, with help, say what those features tell us about how it was made and used. With help, they can write labels and fill in gaps in sentences so that they make sense grammatically and logically. They have to label the picture of the pot and fill in the gaps in the sentences about how the pot was made and used.

Activity sheet 2
This sheet is for children who are learning to answer questions using the evidence provided by an artefact. They can write sentences. They have to write full sentence answers to questions about important features of the pot.

Activity sheet 3
This sheet is for children who (with the help of questions as clues to what to look for) can deduce how an artefact was made and used from its important features. They can write sentences to

answer questions. They have to examine the picture of the pot and then answer questions about it.

Plenary session

Invite the children to share what they have written about the pot. Compare their ideas about the importance of the features such as the handles, spout, lines and burnt patches. Show them pictures of the reconstructions or artists' impressions of Norse homes, and ask them if they can see any clues to how the pot was used. Invite the children to suggest other questions, based on these pictures, which they would like to investigate.

Ideas for support

To help the children to ask and answer questions about Norse artefacts, begin by looking at similar artefacts from today – for example, ceramic items such as jugs, teapots, bowls and ovenware. Ask them what each item is used for and what makes it suitable for that use – for example, a long or short spout or lip for pouring. Look for signs of the use of the artefact such as stains, marks, scratches and the remnants of any previous contents.

Ideas for extension

The children could investigate other artefacts in the same way as they investigated the pot – for example, a piece of jewellery, a coin or a musical instrument.

Investigate place names with Norse components – for example, Birkenhead (*birki*, birch + *hofdi*, headland = headland with birch trees); Copmanthorpe (*kaupmadr*, merchant + *thorp*, village = merchant's village); Mickleby (*mikill*, large + by [*bær*], farm = large farm). Find as many such places as possible and mark them on a map, to which the children can add as they come across others. Use the map to record the parts of Britain where the Norse people settled. A dictionary of place names will be useful.

Linked ICT activities

With the children, discuss things we take for granted today, such as a toothbrush. What would it be like, for a Viking, not to have one? Discuss everyday items such as washing machines, irons, pots and pans, and how technology has helped to improve these and to change the way people live.

Choose small, easy-to-handle items (such as a cup, a teapot, a phone, a torch) to look at with the children. Provide a child-friendly digital camera, ask the children to work in pairs to take a photograph of part of an object. Encourage them to find an unusual angle so that it is difficult to tell what the object is (such as looking down into the cup, or the teapot spout).

Ask the children to use a word processing program to write three sentences as clues to guess what the object is. They should cut and paste the digital image into the document, above their clues.

Print out the text and images for display under the title 'Give us a clue'. Include blank sheets of paper and encourage the children to write down their guesses.

At the end of the week, ask:

• Did the clues help to discover what the objects were?
• Were there any clues in the pictures?

Talk with the children about how archaeologists use clues on artefacts, and in the area around where they were found, to find out what the artefact was.

A Norse loom

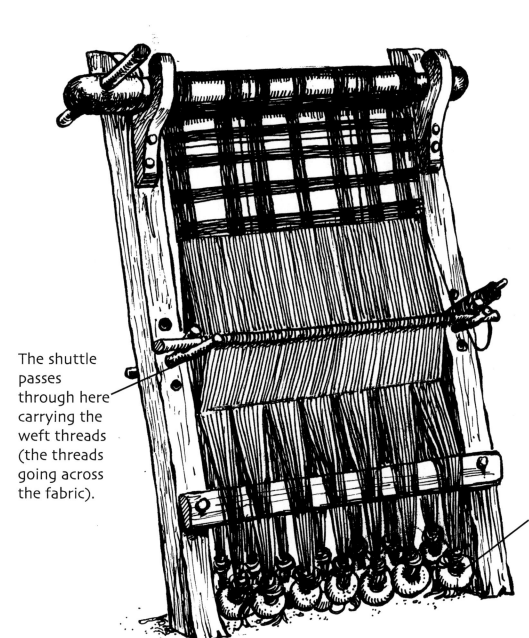

The shuttle passes through here carrying the weft threads (the threads going across the fabric).

Weights made of clay hang from the warp (up and down) threads.

Weaving tablet made of bone.

Tablet weaving: this is how braids were woven.

Norse settlements

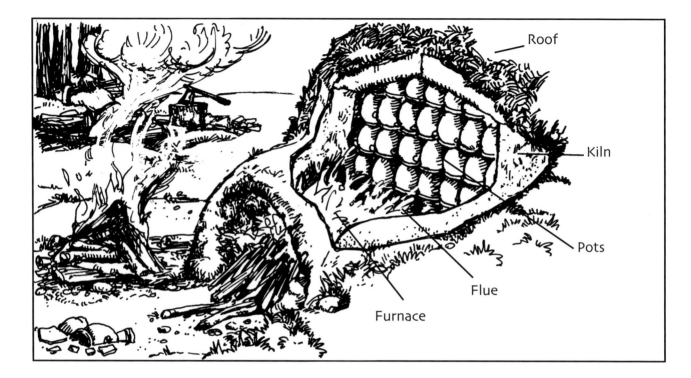

This is how a pot was made by a Norse craftsman in Jórvík:

The potter dug clay from the ground. He mixed it with sand, grass or crushed shells. This helped to bind the clay together. He then shaped the clay into a pot. At one time this was done by hand, but later in the Viking Age a potter's wheel was used. Using a wheel, potters could work much more quickly and make better shaped pots.

To fire the pots the potter dug two shallow pits. He made a rounded roof over one pit, supporting it with stones and covering them with earth and grass. This pit was the kiln (where the pots were placed). They would be stacked one on top of the other, some the right way up and some upside down, to fill the space. Once the kiln

was full the potter sealed the top with wet clay. Only a small passage called a flue was left open.

The flue linked the kiln to the other pit, which was the furnace. The potter piled up wood in the entrance to the flue and lit it. He had to keep it burning for a long time to get it hot enough to fire the pots. Potters learned by practice how long to fire their pots. Once they were fired they had to be left to cool. This could take all night.

The potter would then make a hole and take the pots out through the top. He would sell some in Jórvík but some might be sold to merchants who would take them to other places to sell.

Name _____

Norse settlements

Look at this picture of a pot from the Norse town of Jórvík.
Label the picture. Use the word bank to help you. Fill in the gaps in the sentences.

___

WORD BANK

handles   lines in the clay   smoky patches   spout

The pot has _____ handles. The handles were used for _____
_____
_____

The pot has a spout. The spout was for _____
_____
_____

There are lines in the clay. These might have been made by
_____
_____

There are smoky patches on the pot. These might have been made by
_____
_____

Norse settlements

Look at this picture of a pot from the Norse town of Jórvík.
Answer the questions. Write on the lines in full sentences.

1. What are these and what were they for?

2. What is this and what was it for?

4. What do these smoky patches tell you about how the pot was used?

3. What do these lines tell you about how the pot was made?

1 _____

_____

2 _____

_____

3 _____

_____

4 _____

_____

WORD BANK

burn	cooking	fire	food	handles
heated	hold	lift	pour	spout

PHOTOCOPIABLE

Norse settlements

Look at this picture of a pot from the Norse town of Jórvík.

The pot is made from clay and is about 20 centimetres high and 13 centimetres wide at the base. There are smoky patches on the sides near the bottom.

Handles

Spout

Smoky patches

Lines on clay

Answer these questions. Write your answers on the back of this sheet.

1 Look at the surface pattern of the pot. What do you notice?

2 What does this tell you about how it was made?

3 How do you think the smoky patches got there?

4 What do they tell you about how the pot was used?

5 Why do you think the narrow neck was useful?

6 What do you notice about the handles?

7 What does this tell you about how the pot was used?

8 Describe the spout.

9 What does this tell you about the type of thing that might have been put in the pot?

Alfred the Great

Who was Alfred the Great?

A statue in Wantage in Oxfordshire commemorates the fact that Alfred the Great was born there, in about 849. He was the fifth and youngest son of Æthelwulf, king of the West Saxons (Wessex) and his wife Osburh. His elder brothers died or were killed in battle. Written sources about King Alfred include the *Life of Alfred*, written by Asser (a priest from St David's in Wales who became a member of Alfred's court) and the *Anglo-Saxon Chronicle*.

At that time the Norse invaders had taken over the English kingdoms of Northumbria, East Anglia and Mercia (see Chapter 8) and set up settlements in them. By the time Alfred was 16 years old he was a seasoned warrior, having (after their father's death) fought alongside his brother Æthelred against 'the great heathen host' of Norse invaders who landed in East Anglia in 866. Alfred succeeded Æthelred to the throne of Wessex in 871, after the pair had led their armies into battle several times against the Norsemen. The *Anglo-Saxon Chronicle* records:

'871 Here the raiding-army rode to Reading in Wessex, and 3 days afterwards two jarls rode up-country; then Ealdorman Æthelwulf met them on Englefield *[10 miles west of Reading]* and fought against them there and took the victory; and one of the jarls, whose name was Sidroc, was killed there. Then 4 days later King Æthelred and Alfred, his brother, led a great army there to Reading, and fought against the raiding-army; and great slaughter was made there on either side, and Ealdorman Æthelwulf was killed, and the Danish had possession of the place of slaughter. And 4 days later King Æthelred and Alfred, his brother, fought against the whole raiding-army on Ashdown… And 14 days later King Æthelred and Alfred, his brother, fought against the raiding-army at Basing, and there the Danish took the victory. And two months later Æthelred and Alfred, his brother, fought against the raiding-army at Merton; and they were in two bands, and they put both to flight and for long in the day had the victory; and there was great slaughter on either side, and the

Danish had possession of the place of slaughter … after this fight a great summer-fleet came to Reading … after Easter, King Æthelred died … Then his brother Alfred, Æthelwulf's offspring, succeeded to the kingdom of Wessex.'

The *Anglo-Saxon Chronicle* goes on to record the progress of the 'raiding-army' northwards into Northumbria and even north of the River Tyne with its three Norse kings Guthorm, Oscytel and Anund. Guthorm returned south, settling in Cambridge with a 'great summer army'. Between 876 and 878 Guthorm's army made forays into Wessex but Alfred kept them at bay. Then, in the winter of 878, Guthorm made a decisive attack on Alfred, who was spending the Christmas season at his royal manor at Chippenham with only a small group of followers acting as his bodyguard. He was caught off-guard by Guthorm's army but managed to escape into the fenlands of Somerset. There he hid, making guerrilla attacks on enemy strongholds in the area, from a base near Athelney.

Alfred and the cakes

It was during this time that the famous story of Alfred burning the cakes arose. The story goes that he had taken refuge (incognito) in a herdsman's cottage. While he was sitting by the fire seeing to his weapons, some cakes which the herdsman's wife was baking began to burn. On noticing her burning cakes the woman berated Alfred for letting them burn. Historians have uncovered a different version of this story (in the eleventh-century *Life of St Neot*) in which the woman asked him to keep an eye on the baking, and he did so: 'He was at once obedient to that bad wife, because of necessity he had to be'; the story points to Alfred's humility. The other important difference in this story is that it was loaves and not cakes which were being baked. The significance of loaves is that the Old English word for lord was *hlaf-weard* (loaf-provider), the story being a parable of the relationship of Alfred (as head of the national household) and his subjects, who ate his bread. It made the point, not that Alfred burned some cakes through his preoccupation with his own concerns, but that he looked after the loaves, mindful of his responsibility as king.

Alfred's achievements

In 878 Alfred built a small fortress on the island of Athelney in marshland in Somerset and managed to raise a large local force ready to face Guthorm. By this time Guthorm's army was considerably reduced because many of its members had settled on the estates they had taken over. Instead of Guthorm attacking Alfred, it would be the other way around. He marched to a place in Selwood Forest to a pre-arranged meeting place, known as 'Egbert's Stone' (the location is unknown) and was joined by a large force from Somerset, Wiltshire and Hampshire. The *Life of Alfred* records:

> 'And when they saw the king they received him like one risen from the dead after such great tribulation, and they were filled with great joy.'

Alfred advanced north-eastwards with his army towards Chippenham where Guthorm now had his main encampment. Guthorm's army came out to meet him and they met somewhere on the downs near Edington, just south of Chippenham. The outcome was that the Danes retreated to their camp at Chippenham, with Alfred's army in pursuit. After a siege that lasted a fortnight they sued for peace.

The Danish surrender was formalised in a peace treaty in which the Danes promised to leave Wessex. In addition to this, Guthorm and 30 of his foremost army leaders agreed to accept baptism as Christians. That autumn the Danish army withdrew as promised and in the following year, 879, it moved eastwards and settled in East Anglia. With the treaty Alfred had accepted the presence of the Danes in England and reached an agreement with them as an equal power.

After that, in about 880, Alfred had a coin minted bearing the inscription 'Alfred rex Anglorum' (Alfred king of the English). A later treaty with Guthorm, in about 885–86, defined the limits of the Norse-ruled area of England, which would come to be known as the 'Danelaw'.

Alfred created fortified strongholds called *burhs* to defend his kingdom. Some of them made use of the fortifications from Roman times (for example, Bath, Exeter and Winchester), but others were specially built, with an embankment and ditch surrounding them. We know about these burhs from the Burghal Hidage, a document which was compiled not long after Alfred's death. A 'hide' was a unit of agricultural land sufficient for a peasant family to support itself, and each 'hide' of land had to contribute one man to defend the burh. Each man had to defend just over a metre of wall in times of danger. The sizes of the burhs can be reckoned in 'hides' – for instance, Winchester was rated at 2,400 'hides', which means that its perimeter defences must have measured about 3,000 metres, as can be confirmed from the size of the Roman walls there.

The creation of the Wessex burhs gave Alfred local strength whenever his kingdom was under attack, until he could send a relieving army (the levied fyrd) to help. Because the fyrd tended to disband when men were needed on the farms, Alfred divided the organisation of the fyrd into two relays so that 'always half of its men were at home, half on service'. This sounds like common sense, but at the time it was a completely new idea. It was one of the ways in which Alfred showed that he listened to people's concerns and acted on what he learned.

Another of King Alfred's great achievements was to inspire an upsurge of learning and literature in England, in Anglo-Saxon rather than Latin, despite the fact that, like most other people in England at that time, he had been illiterate during his childhood. He is thought to have urged the compilation of the *Anglo-Saxon Chronicle* in 892 and the first copy is thought to have been written in a scriptorium in his royal palace at Winchester. Alfred also translated Latin works to edify both the clergy and the laity, including *Cura Pastoralis* (Pastoral Care) which he sent to all his bishops, along with a pointer called an 'æstel', which was used for following the text on ceremonial occasions in the churches. The jewelled top of an æstel, inscribed 'AELFRED MEC HEHT GEWYRCAN' ('Alfred had me made'), was found in Athelney and some scholars believe that it might have been from one of Alfred's special æstels.

Alfred has also been called the 'father of the English navy' because he built a fleet of ships to augment the other defences he had set up; it enabled him to anticipate any Viking forces before they could reach land. It was needed in 899, a few months before Alfred's death, when it headed off two fleets which had been making raids on mainland Europe and were approaching the Thames estuary and the River Lyme in Kent.

Alfred the Great

History objectives (Unit 6C)
- To learn about King Alfred and the impact he had.
- To recall, select and organise their knowledge about King Alfred.

Resources

- Maps of Britain showing how it was partitioned before and after the 'Danelaw' was established (see Generic sheet 1 on page 115)
- Pictures of Alfred the Great from contemporary manuscripts or later sources, including a picture of the famous statue of him at Wantage in Oxfordshire and a copy of the inscription on it
- Information books about the life and times of Alfred the Great
- Passages from the *Anglo-Saxon Chronicle* and Asser's *Life of Alfred* (see websites in Useful resources, page 126)
- Generic sheets 1–2 (pages 115–116)
- Activity sheets 1–3 (pages 117–119)

Starting points: *whole class*

The children should first have completed Chapters 1, 8, 9 and 10.

Tell the children that they are going to use information books and pictures to find out about Alfred the Great. Remind them what they have learned about the Norse settlement of Britain and show them a map illustrating how much of Britain (and in particular, England) had been taken over by the Norse invaders who had settled here. Discuss the meanings of 'invade' and 'settle'.

Show the children a picture of the statue of Alfred the Great at Wantage in Oxfordshire and ask them what they think the sculptor was trying to say about Alfred. Read the inscription and point out that the statue was made a long time after Alfred had died. Ask the children what the statue tells them about the things Alfred achieved and what he was like as a king and a person.

Tell the children that we know about Alfred the Great from manuscripts from the time, such as the *Anglo-Saxon Chronicle* and another called the *Life of Alfred*, which was written by a priest named Asser

who joined Alfred's court. Explain the meaning of 'court'. Read some passages from the *Anglo-Saxon Chronicle* and the *Life of Alfred* and ask the children what these texts tell them about Alfred's character. What clues do the texts give as to why he became known as Alfred 'the Great'?

Give the children copies of Generic sheet 2 and read it with them. Reread it and explain any words they do not understand or cannot read (encouraging them to work out the meanings from the context where possible). Tell them additional information about King Alfred (including the other version of the burning of the cakes).

Ask the children to look for the main events of Alfred's life and to suggest headings which could be used to summarise them. Write the headings in chronological order on a large sheet of paper. Ask the children to underline on their copies of the text the key words and phrases which show what Alfred was like as a person and as a king. Discuss the words and phrases they have marked and encourage the children to explain how Alfred became known as 'the Great'.

Summarise how Alfred changed England and what might have happened if he had not established the Danelaw. Draw out his qualities of leadership: he listened to the people, thought about problems and came up with realistic ways in which to solve them.

Tell the children they are now going to find out more about Alfred the Great.

Group activities

Activity sheet 1
This sheet is for children who, with the help of pictures, can express what they have learned from a non-fiction text. They know that the words written in a speech bubble are what someone actually says and, with help, can write what a character might have said in a situation. They have to think about

what Alfred might have said in two situations about which they have read on Generic sheet 2.

Activity sheet 2

This sheet is for children who can identify the facts given in a recount (Generic sheet 2) and can record what they have learned in the form of a chart. They can write sentences to express facts they have found out. They have to read sentences about King Alfred and decide which are true, then write three other facts about King Alfred.

Activity sheet 3

This sheet is for children who can find information from different sources and identify important words and phrases which will help them to answer a question. They are learning to write meaningful notes. They have to write their own summary of why Alfred was called 'the Great' by using information sources, which they also have to record.

Plenary session

Invite the children who completed Activity sheet 1 to read what King Alfred might have said in the two situations that are depicted on the sheet. Ask the others to listen and to give their opinions about what King Alfred might have said.

Invite the children who completed Activity sheet 2 to share the answers they gave and the sentences they wrote to give facts about King Alfred. Refer to Generic sheet 2 to check the accuracy of what they wrote. Ask them what they think made Alfred 'great'.

Ask the children what they think would have happened if Alfred had not defeated Guthorm. Ask them what England might have been like today and who might be ruling the country.

Ideas for support

To help the children to understand the impact of King Alfred's actions, they could enact the events of King Alfred's life. Encourage them to stop at important points – for example, when Alfred's army held Guthorm's army under siege. Ask the children about the options Alfred had. Discuss the possible courses of action and what might have happened if Alfred had made different choices (such as massacring the Norse army or forcing them to leave England).

Another important point at which to stop is when

Alfred hears that men from his army keep deserting their posts: the children could enact a scene in which a local leader comes to tell Alfred that he has hardly any men left to defend the walls of the burh because it is harvest time and many of the men have gone home to tend to their crops. List the options he had and discuss what might have happened in each case.

Ideas for extension

Ask the children to find out about the towns in England which were once Alfred the Great's burhs. If possible, visit one of them and find out about its past; look for remains of Alfred's fortifications and written records of the town. Examples of the remains of Alfred's burhs include Burgh Hill near Hurst Green, Chisbury, Exeter, Wallingford, Wareham, Winchester, Witham and Worcester. You could help the children to mark the locations of Alfred's burhs on an outline map of England and to show how people in England were protected by them (no one was more than 20 miles from a burh).

Help the children to find out about Alfred the Great's navy – the types of ships he built, their sizes and the men who sailed them.

Show the children pictures of the 'Alfred Jewel' in the Ashmolean Museum, Oxford, and the only surviving copy of Alfred's *Cura Pastoralis*. Help the children to find out about Alfred's influence on religion in England.

Linked ICT activities

Ask the children which famous historical people they have heard of. Discuss what the people are famous for. Tell the children that, working in pairs, they are going to research a famous person. They can use CD-Roms, but check with your LEA guidelines on children using search engines (some LEAs provide them for schools) before asking the children to search the internet for information.

Provide a fact file sheet for each person, with a list of questions:

- What was X famous for?
- When was X born?
- When did X die?
- How did X die?
- Describe X's appearance.

Five questions should be plenty for the children to start with, but you can add more questions later.

Prepare a database using *Find IT* or *Information Workshop* (see Useful resources on page 126). Show the children how to enter their information. The database will become a class fact file for famous people in history.

Alfred the Great

A map showing the boundary of the Danelaw

Alfred the Great

In the year 849 Osburh, the wife of Æthelwulf, king of Wessex, gave birth to her fifth son – Alfred.

Wessex was the only part of England which was not ruled by the Norsemen. The people of Wessex called them 'heathens' because they were not Christians. Alfred was brought up as a Christian. He was even taken on pilgrimages to Rome.

By the time Alfred was 16 his father had died and only one of his brothers was still alive – Æthelred, who became king. Alfred fought alongside Æthelred in many battles against the Norsemen. Æthelred was killed at one of these battles and Alfred became king of Wessex.

Alfred kept a close watch on any Norsemen in and around Wessex and led his army against them whenever trouble looked likely. Then one Christmas, while Alfred was celebrating at home, a band of Norsemen led by King Guthorm rushed in. Alfred managed to escape with some of his men. He went into hiding. One place where he hid was a herdsman's cottage. The herdsman's wife is said to have scolded him for letting her cakes burn while he was sitting nearby.

Before long Alfred gathered an army and persuaded others to join him against the Norsemen. This time Alfred surprised Guthorm and held him and his army under siege in their stronghold. When they were forced to come out, Alfred did not harm them but talked to Guthorm about how they could live alongside one another in peace. He agreed that the Norsemen could rule part of Britain (to be called the 'Danelaw') but they must not try to take any more. He also persuaded them to become Christians.

Alfred then learned to read. He even wrote books, in Old English. Most books at the time were written in Latin by monks or priests. He is said to have begun the famous book which lists the main events of early English history – the *Anglo-Saxon Chronicle*.

Then Alfred set about defending his land. He built fortified settlements called burhs and said that each man there had to defend part of the walls. In that way the whole burh could be defended. Alfred also tackled the problem of men deserting his army during busy times on their farms. He divided the army into relays: one relay would be on duty while the other was at home.

His other way of defending his land was to build a fleet of ships to stop Viking attacks. This fleet kept a large Viking army away during the year Alfred died (899).

Alfred the Great

In the speech bubble write what Alfred might have said.
Choose from:

I'm going to kill you all.	Go back to your own land.	Now we can have revenge.	Let us talk.

Alfred with his army outside the stronghold of Guthorm.

What two things did King Guthorm promise? Write in the speech bubbles.
Choose from:

We shall rule the Danelaw and keep off your lands.	We shall go back to our country.	I shall give you gold if you don't kill me.	We shall become Christians.

King Guthorm and King Alfred and their officials.

Name _____

Alfred the Great

Reread the story of King Alfred on Generic sheet 2.

Now read the sentences below and tick those that are true.

Alfred became king because he was the king of Wessex's eldest son.	
The Norsemen ruled all of England except Wessex.	
Alfred lived in Rome.	
Alfred's brother became king.	
Alfred helped his brother in battles against the Norsemen.	
Alfred killed his brother so that he could be king.	
Guthorm was a Norse king.	
Guthorm captured Alfred.	
Guthorm tried to capture Alfred but Alfred escaped.	
Alfred gathered an army and overcame Guthorm and his army.	
Alfred killed Guthorm and his army.	
Alfred made an agreement with Guthorm and his army.	
Alfred said that Guthorm had to go back to his own country.	
Alfred said that the Norsemen could rule part of England.	

On the back of this sheet, write three other facts about King Alfred.

Alfred the Great

Use information books and pictures to find out why King Alfred was called 'the Great'. Fill in the table.

The question I am trying to answer: Why was King Alfred called 'the Great'? Where I found the answer:	
Books	CD-Roms
Pictures	Websites
What I found out (make notes)	
The answer to the question	

Glossary

Chapter 1

asylum seekers People who leave their country and go to another to seek protection from persecution.

emigrants People who leave the country where they were born or grew up to go and settle in another.

emigrate To leave the country where you were born or grew up to go and settle in another.

immigrants People who come to settle in a country from another.

immigrate To come and settle in a country from another.

invade To go into a place in a hostile way in large numbers or with an armed force.

invasion Entering a country or area with armed forces and in a hostile way.

persecution Being harassed, oppressed or harmed because of one's beliefs.

refugees People who have to leave their country because of war, persecution, political troubles or a natural disaster, and who no longer have a home.

settle To make one's home somewhere.

Chapter 2

amphitheatre A circular or oval arena in which spectators watched gladiatorial fights and other entertainments.

amphora A clay jar for storing wine or oil.

archaeologist Someone who finds out about the past by excavating, examining and testing remains.

basilica A building used for public ceremonies and meetings.

Briton Someone who lives in Britain; in Roman times one of the peoples (including the Celts) who lived in Britain when the Romans invaded.

Caledonia Scotland.

cavalry Soldiers who fought on horseback.

Celt A member of the groups of ancient peoples of Western Europe.

centurion A Roman soldier in charge of between 80 and 100 soldiers.

Claudius Claudius I (10BC–AD54): the fourth Roman emperor, who took part in the campaign to conquer Britain in AD43.

conquer To take possession of a place and people by force of arms.

conquest The act of taking possession of a place by force of arms.

daub Mud or clay used for plastering the walls of houses.

emperor The ruler of an empire.

empire A large territory made up of other countries which have been taken over, and are ruled by, the conqueror.

forum A marketplace or public meeting place near public buildings in a town.

governor Someone in charge of an area, for example, a part of the Roman Empire.

hypocaust A central heating system used by the Romans. Hot air from a furnace outside the house flowed through ducts beneath the stone floors to heat the rooms.

invade To go into a place in a hostile way in large numbers or with an armed force.

Latin The language of the ancient Romans.

legion A main unit of the Roman army made up of about 3,000 to 6,000 soldiers.

legionary A soldier in a legion.

mosaic A pattern or picture made up from very small pieces of stone, glass or other hard material and used mainly on floors and walls.

revolt An uprising against the ruling group.

settle To make one's home somewhere.

toga A loose garment, made from a large piece of cloth and worn by Roman men. It was draped over one shoulder.

villa A large country house or a farm made up of a house and outbuildings.

wattle Twigs and branches woven to make fences or frameworks for the walls of houses.

Chapter 3

archaeologist Someone who finds out about the past by excavating, examining and testing remains.

Catuvellauni A British tribe whose lands were just north of the River Thames.

cavalry Soldiers who fought on horseback.

colonia (plural coloniae) A settlement for retired legionaries.

Dio Cassius (c.AD150–235) The Roman historian who wrote *History of Rome*.

emperor The ruler of the Roman Empire.

general A soldier in charge of an army.

governor Someone in charge of an area, for example, a part of the Roman Empire.

Iceni A British tribe whose lands were in the area now covered mainly by East Anglia (to the north of the Catuvellauni and Trinovantes).

infantry Foot soldiers.

legion A body of 3,000 to 6,000 infantry in the Roman army, usually accompanied by cavalry.

legionary A soldier in a legion.

mantle A cloak of thick cloth, fastened on the shoulder with a brooch.

procurator A Roman officer who collected taxes, paid the troops and looked after the treasury of a province of the Roman Empire, such as Britain.

Suetonius Paulinus The Roman governor of Britain at the time of Boudica's revolt.

Tacitus (Publius or Gaius Cornelius Tacitus, c.AD55–120). The Roman historian who wrote *Historiae* and *Annals*, about the Roman Empire.

torc A thick, twisted metal neck band, usually made of gold or bronze.

Trinovantes A British tribe whose lands were north of the Thames and east of those of the Catuvellauni.

Watling Street Originally the Roman road running from near London through St Albans to Wroxeter in Shropshire.

Chapter 4

amphitheatre A circular or oval arena in which spectators watched gladiatorial fights and other entertainments.

archaeologist Someone who finds out about the past by excavating, examining and testing remains.

basilica A building used for public ceremonies and meetings.

bathhouse A public building where people took hot and cold baths and socialised.

caldarium A very hot room in a Roman bathhouse.

emperor The ruler of an empire.

empire A large territory made up of other countries that have been taken over by one ruling country.

forum A marketplace or public meeting place near public buildings in a town.

frigidarium A cold room in a Roman bathhouse containing a pool of icy cold water in which people took a refreshing cold dip after a hot bath.

governor Someone in charge of an area – for example, a part of the Roman Empire.

gymnasium An exercise room in a Roman bathhouse, where people could wrestle, lift weights, play ball games or take part in other forms of exercise.

hypocaust A central heating system used by the Romans. Hot air from a furnace outside the house flowed through ducts beneath the stone floors to heat the rooms.

Latin The language of the ancient Romans.

latrine A lavatory.

legion A main unit of the Roman army made up of about 3,000 to 6,000 soldiers.

sudatorium A sweating room in a Roman bathhouse in which people relaxed after a hot bath and before a cold dip.

temple A place for the communal worship of gods, which was often dedicated to a particular god.

tepidarium A warm room in a Roman bathhouse, where people relaxed after oils had been applied to, and then scraped off, their skin.

villa A large country house or a farm made up of a house and outbuildings.

Chapter 5

Angles A Germanic tribe who invaded and settled in Britain in the fifth century.

Anglo-Saxons The name given to the people of Britain after the Angles, Saxons and Jutes had settled here.

archaeologist Someone who finds out about the past by excavating, examining and testing remains.

barbarian A word used for the peoples such as the Picts, Saxons and Scots, who launched attacks on Britain during the fourth century.

Gildas A monk who lived c.493–570 and wrote *The Overthrow and Conquest of Britain*.

Hengist and Horsa Brothers who, according to Gildas, led a Saxon invasion of England in AD449, but who may have been legendary characters.

Jutes A Germanic tribe who invaded and settled in Britain in the fifth century.

kingdom An area ruled by a king or queen.

loom weights Weights (often made of stone in Anglo-Saxon times) attached to the bottom of bunches of threads hanging from a vertical weaving loom to keep them taut.

Offa King of Mercia (757–796).

Offa's Dyke An earthwork wall built by Offa along the border between Mercia and Wales.

Picts ('Painted people') The early inhabitants of Scotland.

Saxons A Germanic tribe who invaded and settled in Britain in the fifth century.

Vortigern (active from 425–*c*.455). The leader of the Britons who led the resistance against Saxon invasions in the fifth century.

Chapter 6

Anglo-Saxons The name given to the people of Britain after the Angles, Saxons and Jutes had settled here.

archaeologist Someone who finds out about the past by excavating, examining and testing remains.

artefact Something made by people.

cemetery A place where the dead are buried.

cremation The burning of the body after the person has died.

dowser Someone who searches for hidden water or mineral deposits by passing a forked branch (often hazel) over the surface of the ground; the stick dips suddenly if the material is present.

drinking horn An animal's horn, hollowed out and sometimes richly decorated, which was used as a drinking vessel in Anglo-Saxon times.

dynasty A family of many generations – 'dynasty' is usually used for a royal family.

excavate To dig in order to find out about the past.

kingdom An area ruled by a king or queen.

Rædwald (reigned *c*.617–*c*.625). An Anglo-Saxon king of the Wuffing dynasty, who is thought to have been buried in, or commemorated by, Mound 1 at Sutton Hoo. He became overlord of Britain after defeating Æthelfrith, king of Northumbria, at the Battle of the River Idle, not far from Bawtry, near Doncaster (*c*.617).

rivet A type of nail or bolt for fastening together sheets or planks of material such as wood or metal.

Wuffing An Anglo-Saxon royal dynasty of East Anglia.

Chapter 7

Anglo-Saxons The name given to the people of Britain after the Angles, Saxons and Jutes had settled here.

archaeologist Someone who finds out about the past by excavating, examining and testing remains.

artefact Something made by people.

Bede (the 'Venerable Bede', *c*.673–735). An Anglo-Saxon scholar, historian and monk from near Durham who was ordained at the monastery of Jarrow, where he wrote *Ecclesiastical History of the English People*.

Beowulf An Old English epic poem from about the eighth century, based on Norse legends merged with historical events of the early sixth century in Denmark. The main character, Beowulf, was the son of the Danish king Scyld and a nephew of King Hygelac of the Geats of the south-eastern coast of Sweden.

boss The raised piece in the centre of a shield, often highly decorative, and used for knocking down opponents.

cemetery A place where the dead are buried.

cloisonné Enamelware in which the colours in the pattern are separated by narrow strips of gold.

cremation The burning of the body after the person has died.

dynasty A family of many generations – 'dynasty' is usually used for a royal family.

excavate To dig in order to find out about the past.

filigree Ornamental work with beads or precious stones, with fine twisted or plaited wire (usually of gold or silver) soldered to form a delicate openwork design.

garnet A red gemstone.

hilt The handle of a sword.

kingdom An area ruled by a king or queen.

millefiori (literally 'a thousand flowers'). A type of ornamental glass made by fusing together glass rods of different sizes and colours. The material is then cut into decorative shapes, such as flowers, and embedded into metal or glass.

numismatist Someone who studies coins.

pagan This used to mean someone who was not a Christian.

pommel The raised, rounded part at the top of the handle of a sword.

Rædwald (reigned *c*.617–*c*.625). An Anglo-Saxon king of the Wuffing dynasty, who is thought to have been buried in, or commemorated by, Mound 1 at Sutton Hoo. He became overlord of Britain after defeating Æthelfrith, king of Northumbria, at the Battle of the River Idle, not far from Bawtry, near Doncaster (*c*.617).

rivet A type of nail or bolt for fastening together sheets or planks of material such as wood or metal.

scabbard The sheath or covering for a sword.

Wuffing An Anglo-Saxon royal dynasty of East Anglia.

Chapter 8

Anglo-Saxon Chronicle A list of events in England from the year AD494 to 1154, with a summary prologue from AD1.

Anglo-Saxons The name given to the people of Britain after the Angles, Saxons and Jutes had settled here.

conquer To take over a people by force of arms.

Danegeld Money the Anglo-Saxons paid to the Vikings to be left in peace.

dynasty A family of many generations – 'dynasty' is usually used for a royal family.

ealdorman An elder or chief of a group of people.

Ealhere An ealdorman of Kent who was killed in 852.

Ecgfrith King of Northumbria (killed in 685) who set up the monastery at Jarrow.

Eorwic The Anglo-Saxon name for York.

heathen This used to mean someone who was not a Christian.

Huda An ealdorman of Surrey who was killed in 852.

invade To go into a place in a hostile way in large numbers or with an armed force.

Jarrow A place in Northumbria where there was a monastery.

Jórvík The Viking name for York.

kingdom An area ruled by a king or queen.

Lindisfarne An island (Holy Island) off the coast of Northumberland on which St Aidan had set up a church and monastery in the 630s.

minster A church (usually a church with a monastery).

monastery A community of monks.

monk A religious man who lives in a community of monks and obeys the rules of that group. In Anglo-Saxon Britain monks were all Christians.

Norse From Scandinavian countries such as Denmark, Norway and Sweden.

portent An omen or warning.

saga A historical story based on real people, places and events, but in which parts have been invented. 'Saga' is usually used for the stories about heroic events of the past which were written in Iceland in the thirteenth century.

settle To make one's home somewhere.

trade To buy, sell or exchange goods.

Vikings A name given to the Norsemen from Denmark, Norway and Sweden who attacked Britain and went on trading expeditions to other European countries. To the people of those countries, however, being a 'viking' was something which young men might do for a few summers: they went on raiding expeditions to prove their strength and courage and to gather wealth.

Chapter 9

clinker-built Built with planks that overlap downwards and are fixed with rivets or nails.

draught The depth of water a ship needs to let it float freely.

galley A low, flat, single-decked ship that is rowed.

hull The body of a ship.

invade To go into a place in a hostile way in large numbers or with an armed force.

keel One of the main structures of a ship, extending along the bottom from front to back.

kingdom An area ruled by a king or queen.

knörr A Norse merchant ship.

longship A type of Norse warship.

mast A vertical pole on a ship to which the sail is fixed.

Norse From Scandinavian countries: Denmark, Norway and Sweden.

prow The pointed part of the front of a ship.

rigging The ropes which support a ship's mast or are attached to the sail.

rivet A type of nail or bolt for fastening together sheets or planks of material such as wood or metal.

rudder A broad piece of wood or metal hinged vertically at or near the stern of a ship for steering.

saga A historical story based on real people, places and events, but in which parts have been invented. 'Saga' is usually used for the stories about heroic events of the past which were written in Iceland in the thirteenth century.

settle To make one's home somewhere.

starboard (from 'steerboard', meaning rudder-side). The right-hand side of a ship (looking forward).

stern The back end of a ship.

strake One of the planks used in making the hull of a ship.

trade To buy, sell or exchange goods.

Vikings A name given to Norsemen from Denmark, Norway and Sweden who attacked Britain and went on trading expeditions to other European countries. To the people of those countries, however, being a 'viking' was something which young men might do for a few summers: they went on raiding expeditions to prove their strength and courage and to gather wealth.

Chapter 10

amber A yellow fossil resin which can be polished and used for making jewellery.

antler The horny branching growth on the heads of animals such as deer.

archaeologist Someone who finds out about the past by excavating, examining and testing remains.

artefact Something made by people.

bargeboards Wooden facings fixed below the eaves of a roof or along a gable end.

conquer To take possession of a place and people by force of arms.

conquest The act of taking possession of a place by force of arms.

daub Mud or clay used for plastering the walls of houses.

excavate To dig in order to find out about the past.

furnace A very hot fire.

invade To go into a place in a hostile way in large numbers or with an armed force.

kiln A very hot oven for firing pots.

kingdom An area ruled by a king or queen.

last A foot-shaped block on which shoes are made.

lathe A tool which was used for turning rounded wooden artefacts such as bowls while the wood-worker cut them.

loom weights Weights (often made of stone in Anglo-Saxon times) attached to the bottom of bunches of threads hanging from a vertical weaving loom to keep them taut.

lyre A stringed musical instrument.

Norse From Scandinavian countries: Denmark, Norway and Sweden.

privy Lavatory.

quern A large round stone with which grain was ground.

saga A historical story based on real people, places and events, but in which parts have been invented. 'Saga' is usually used for the stories about heroic events of the past which were written in Iceland in the thirteenth century.

settle To make one's home somewhere.

tallow Animal fat used for making candles.

trade To buy, sell or exchange goods.

Vikings A name given to Norsemen from Denmark, Norway and Sweden who attacked Britain and went on trading expeditions to other European countries. To the people of those countries, however, being a 'viking' was something which young men might do for a few summers: they went on raiding expeditions to prove their strength and courage and to gather wealth.

wattle Twigs and branches woven to make fences or frameworks for the walls of houses.

Chapter 11

Anglo-Saxon Chronicle A list of events in England from the year AD494 to 1154, with a summary prologue from AD1.

Anglo-Saxons The name given to the people of Britain after the Angles, Saxons and Jutes had settled here.

Athelney The place in Somerset where King Alfred built his stronghold while he was in hiding.

burh A fortified town set up by King Alfred. Men living in burhs had to defend a section of the walls.

conquer To take possession of a place and people by force of arms.

conquest The act of taking possession of a place by force of arms.

Danelaw The part of England ruled by the Norsemen after AD886.

Guthorm (sometimes called 'Guthrum', died 890). Danish king of East Anglia who drove King Alfred into hiding in Athelney. He was defeated by Alfred at the battle of Edington, Wiltshire, in 878.

heathen This used to mean someone who was not a Christian.

hide The amount of land needed to support a family. Each burh was measured in hides.

invade To go into a place in a hostile way in large numbers or with an armed force.

kingdom An area ruled by a king or queen.

Latin The language of the Romans which was still used in churches and for books (because they were written mainly by monks and priests) at the time of Alfred the Great.

Norse From Scandinavian countries such as Denmark, Norway and Sweden.

settle To make one's home somewhere.

Vikings A name given to Norsemen from Denmark, Norway and Sweden who attacked Britain and went on trading expeditions to other European countries. To the people of those countries, however, being a 'viking' was something which young men might do for a few summers: they went on raiding expeditions to prove their strength and courage and to gather wealth.

Wessex The kingdom of the West Saxons, of which Alfred became king when his brother Æthelred died.

Useful resources

Books and electronic publications

Abels, R (1998) *Alfred the Great*. Harlow: Longman.

Civardi, A and Amery, H (1990) *Time Travellers: Viking Raiders*. London: Usborne.

Cottle, B (1967) *The Penguin Dictionary of Surnames*. London: Penguin.

Crossley-Holland, K (1982, 1999) *Beowulf*. Oxford: Oxford University Press.

Crummy, P (1997) *City of Victory*. Colchester: Colchester Archaeological Trust.

Curtis, E and Davidson, K (1996) *Settlers of Scotland*. London: Hodder and Stoughton.

Daily Mail (1996) *Century: 100 Amazing Years* (CD-Rom).

Guy, J (2002) *Roman Life*. Tunbridge Wells: Ticktock Entertainment.

Hall, J and Merrifield, R (2000) *Roman London*. London: Museum of London.

Haywood, J (2000) *Encyclopedia of the Viking Age*. London: Thames and Hudson.

Langley, A and de Souza, P (1996) *The Roman News*. London: Walker.

Lee, C (ed.) (1997) *This Sceptred Isle*. London: BBC/Penguin.

Magnusson, M (2000) *The Vikings*. Stroud: Tempus.

McAleary, T (1999) *Life in Roman Britain*. London: English Heritage.

Mills, A D (1998) *Oxford English Place Names*. Oxford: Oxford University Press.

Richards, J D (1991) *Viking Age England*. London: English Heritage/Book Club Associates.

Sawyer, P (ed.) (1997) *The Oxford Illustrated History of the Vikings*. Oxford: Oxford University Press.

Schama, S (2000) *A History of Britain Vol 1*. London: BBC Books.

Scullard, H H (1979) *Roman Britain: Outpost of the Empire*. London: Thames and Hudson.

Sealey, P R (1997) *The Boudican Revolt Against Rome*. Risborough: Shire Archaeology.

Serraillier, I (1954) *Beowulf the Warrior*. Montoursville, Philadelphia: Bethlehem Books.

Stoppleman, M (1994) *Here? Anglo-Saxon Village*. London: A & C Black.

Swanton, M (1996) (ed.) *The Anglo-Saxon Chronicle*. London: Dent.

Waters, G (2002) *Usborne Puzzle Adventures: Time Train to Ancient Rome*. London: Usborne.

Welch, M (1992) *Anglo-Saxon England*. London: English Heritage/Batsford.

Williams, B (1994) *History of Britain: Roman Britain*. Oxford: Heinemann.

Williams, B (1997) *History of Britain: Life in a Viking Town*. Oxford: Heinemann.

Museums

Ashmolean Museum, Beaumont Street, Oxford OX1 2PH. Tel: 01865 278 000
www.ashmol.ox.ac.uk

The British Museum, Great Russell Street, London WC1B 3DG. Tel: 020 7323 8299
www.british-museum.ac.uk

Castle Museum, Colchester, Castle Park, Colchester CO1 1YG. Tel: 01206 282 939
www.colchestermuseum.org.uk

City Museum, Winchester, Hampshire SO23 7DW. Tel: 01962 848 269
www.winchester.gov.uk/arts_museums/museums/citymuseum.shtml

Jórvík Centre, Coppergate, York YO1 9W. Tel: 01904 643 211
jorvik@jvcyork.demon.co.uk
www.jorvik-viking-centre.co.uk

Museum of London, 150 London Wall, London EC2Y 5HN. Tel: 020 7600 3699
www.museum-london.org.uk

Sutton Hoo Visitor Centre, Woodbridge, Suffolk IP12 3DJ. Tel: 01394 389 700
www.nationaltrust.org.uk

Verulamium Museum, St Michael's Street, St Albans, Herts AL3 4SW. Tel: 01727 751 810
www.stalbansmuseums.org.uk

West Stow Country Park and Anglo-Saxon Village, Visitor Centre, Icklingham Road, West Stow, Bury St Edmunds, Suffolk IP28 6HG. Tel: 01284 728 718.
www.stedmunds.co.uk/lifestyle/west-stow.html

Websites

Roman Britain
www.ukans.edu/history
www.roman_history.org
www.roman-britain.org

Nova Online Lost Empires
www.pbs.org/wgbh/nova/lostempires/roman

The Antonine Wall
www.britainexpress.com/History/roman/antonine-wall.htm

Hadrian's Wall
www.britainexpress.com/History/Hadrian%27s_Wall.htm

Angelcynn
www.angelcynn.org.uk

BBC Education: the Anglo-Saxons
www.bbc.co.uk/education/anglosaxons/index.shtml

School History
www.schoolhistory.co.uk/primarylinks/anglo-saxons.html

Regia Anglorum
www.regia.org

West Stow
www.geocities.com/Athens/2471/weststow.html

The Saxon calendar, The Labours of the Months
www.trin.cam.ac.uk/sdk13/ASCalendar/ASCalendar.html

Sutton Hoo Society
www.suttonhoo.org

The National Trust, Sutton Hoo
www.nationaltrust.org.uk/places/suttonhoo

The Sutton Hoo Room
http://csis.pace.edu/grendel/projs4a/sutton.htm

Lothene (Vikings in Scotland)
www.lothene.demon.co.uk

24-Hour Museum
www.24hourmuseum.org.uk/trlout/HOB01.html

Viking ships
www.stemnet.nf.ca/CITE/vikingships.htm

The Briese-Bane Viking Ships Information Centre
http://homepage.powerup.com.au/~rhayes/vikingb/vikshipl.htm

Danish Viking Ships
www.copenhagenpictures.dk/vik_skib.html

Vestrus Viking Ships
www.vestrusvikingships.org/faering.htm

Hjemkomst Viking Ship, Heritage Hjemkomst Interpretive Center, Minnesota
www.hjemkomst-center.com/ship/main.htm

The Burghal Hidage
www.ogdoad.force9.co.uk/alfred/alfhidage.htm

Alfred the Great
www.mirror.org/people/ken.roberts/king.alfred.html

The *Anglo-Saxon Chronicle*
http://sunsite.berkeley.edu/OMACL/Anglo

Life of Alfred by Asser
http://sunsite.berkeley.edu/OMACL/KingAlfred
www.bartleby.com/211/0601.html
http://britishhistory.about.com/cs/saxons

Replica artefacts

For Jórvík artefacts:
TTS Group Ltd, Nunn Brook Road, Huthwaite, Sutton-in-Ashfield, NG17 2HU. Tel 01623 447 800
www.tts-group.co.uk

Resources recommended for linked ICT activities

Software
Dazzle Granada Learning/SEMERC, Granada Television, Quay Street, Manchester M60 9EA. Tel: 0161 827 2927 www.granada-learning.com
Find IT Database ACTIS Ltd, Rutland Mills, Market Street, Ilkeston, Derbyshire DE7 5RY. Tel: 0115 944 8330 www.actis.co.uk
Information Workshop Granada Learning/SEMERC, Granada Television, Quay Street, Manchester M60 9EA. Tel: 0161 827 2927 www.granada-learning.com
Local Studies R-E-M Software, Great Western House, Langport, Somerset TA10 9YU. Tel: 01458 254 700 www.r-e-m.co.uk
Microsoft Paintbrush part of the Windows package on a PC
Microsoft Publisher from any software supplier

Textease 2000 Softease Ltd, Market Place, Ashbourne, Derbyshire DE6 1ES. Tel: 01335 343 421, Fax: 01335 343 422; www.softease.com

Websites
www.ask.co.uk 'Ask Jeeves' search engine
www.bbc.co.uk/education/anglosaxons
www.bbc.co.uk/history/ancient/vikings lots of general information on Vikings
www.bbc.co.uk/schools/romans
www.channel4.com/history/timeteam
www.english-heritage.org.uk
www.google.co.uk easy-to-use search engine (but first check with your LEA guidelines on children using search engines)
www.hunterian.gla.ac.uk/Archives/vikings easy to navigate; really useful resources

www.pastforward.co.uk/vikings good source of information on Viking ships
www.stedmundsbury.gov.uk/histmain.htm
www.stemnet.nf.ca/CITE/vikingships.htm easy to navigate; lots of useful information
www.suttonhoo.org
www.thebritishmuseum.ac.uk/compass type 'Vikings' into the quick search to see many images of Norse artefacts
www.vikingsonline.org.uk some very interesting images from this re-enactment society in the resources section image gallery

Digital camera
Digital Dream 'L'Elegante' digital camera for children: TAG Learning. Tel: 01474 357 350, Fax 01474 537 887; www.taglearning.co.uk